POWERFUL PRAYERS FOR YOUR MARRIAGE

DAVID AND HEATHER KOPP

WATERBROOK
PRESS

POWERFUL PRAYERS FOR YOUR MARRIAGE
PUBLISHED BY WATERBROOK PRESS
2375 Telstar Drive, Suite 160
Colorado Springs, Colorado 80920
A division of Random House, Inc.

ISBN 1-57856-851-X

Printed in the United States of America
2004

15 14 13 12 11 10 9 8 7 6 5 4 3 2 1

Dedicated to Mary L. Kopp

Thanks for praying, Mom.
Philippians 1:6

Contents

Foreword

I wonder what deep needs you and your family face today. You may be looking for answers to pressing financial or health concerns. You may have a child or loved one who needs a spiritual awakening. Your marriage may need a fresh wind of understanding, forgiveness, and love. You may want to personally experience more of the nearness of Christ in your daily life.

Friend, your prayers are *meant* to make great things happen. And the very fact that you're holding this book and reading this page tells me that you are about to experience more truth and power, more answers to prayer for yourself and those you love than ever before.

Why would I think that, you wonder?

Because picking up this book indicates something extremely important about you, I believe. It strongly suggests that you are ready to take God at His Word and expect life-changing answers when you pray.

As surprising as it may sound, that desire sets you apart from many believers today. In fact, it's been my observation that millions of contemporary Christians really, honestly *don't* believe that prayer is meant to change things in a big way. They might concede that prayer can help your emotional state or give you more spiritual enlightenment. But prayer that results in observable, even miraculous, answers for us, our families, and our world on a *regular* basis? That kind of belief seems naïve to them, or too self-centered, or just too good to be true.

Interestingly, Jesus Himself made the most astonishing statements in the whole Bible about prayer. For example, He said, "If you abide in Me, and My words abide in you, you will ask what you desire, and it shall be done for you" (John 15:7, NKJV).

As a follower of Jesus, I believe prayer that expects answers is simply faith at work. And faith always begins with taking God at His Word.

Approximately three thousand years ago, one of history's great no-bodies decided to take God at His Word. His name was Jabez. When he looked at himself and his circumstances, he saw no reason to hope, no opportunity for change, and certainly no sign that a miracle might be in store. Yet he prayed a simple, bold prayer that is still changing lives today. You can read his mini-biography and his request in 1 Chronicles 4:9-10. Here is what Jabez prayed, according to the *New King James* translation:

> "Oh that You would bless me indeed, and enlarge my territory, that Your hand would be with me, and that You would keep me from evil, that I may not cause pain!"

The next sentence records what happened:

> "So God granted him what he requested."

Talk about results! Each of his four requests brought Jabez answers from God, honor in his generation, and an impact among millions who are still learning from his example.

Obviously, how we pray *does* make a difference, and there's much to be learned from Jabez's prayer. But right now I want you to notice one thing in particular: *Jabez desperately wanted to receive what God was waiting to give.*

Let me show you what I mean:

- Jabez cried out for more blessing. God had already promised to bless Abraham and his descendants, and the whole world through them. (See Genesis 12:1-3.)
- Jabez begged for more territory. God had already commanded Moses to conquer and fully occupy all the lands He had given to

Israel. (See Deuteronomy 1:8.)

- Jabez pleaded for more of God's power. God had already promised Joshua His presence and power. (See Joshua 1:1-9.)
- And Jabez called out to God for protection from sin and evil. God had already revealed to Israel the choice between "life and good, death and evil" and how to live if they wanted to receive His blessing and protection. (See Deuteronomy 30:15-16.)

It's quite possible that the reason God granted Jabez's requests was that, long after others in Israel had stop expecting very much from God, Jabez still wanted—and asked for—all that God in His goodness had promised!

I've heard from thousands of modern-day Jabezes who are seeing extraordinary results as they pray this scriptural prayer. Not because the words are in any way magical, mind you, but because these individuals are wholeheartedly asking—perhaps for the first time—for God's answers in God's way.

That's where the Powerful Prayers series can help you. Carefully, conscientiously, and expectantly praying Scripture is one way we can know that, as Paul said, we "have the mind of Christ" (1 Corinthians 2:16). Written by my good friends and coworkers David and Heather Kopp, these honest and personal prayers can help you hear God's heart while expressing the deepest desires of your own.

If you're ready to know God better and ask for His very best, this book is for you. I highly recommend it.

May God bless you as you reach for a larger life for His glory and expect greater blessings from Him than you have ever imagined before. Your God is that good, and that ready to answer.

—BRUCE WILKINSON, author, *The Prayer of Jabez*

An Invitation

The prayer book you are holding is composed almost entirely of Scripture-based prayers, personalized for a husband or wife. It is especially for you if you've ever thought, *My prayer life is stuck. If I bore myself, how must God be feeling?* Or, *My prayers for my marriage seem weak and ineffective. How can I pray with strength and confidence?*

Intentionally praying Scripture can bring a whole new dimension to our prayer experience. As a pastor from an earlier time wrote, "Through the Bible God talks to us, and through prayer we talk to God. Few of us are ever prepared to speak to God, until God has spoken to us by His Word."[1] By reflecting attentively on Scripture as we pray, we let the words and desires of Christ dwell richly within us (Col. 3:16). And we understand in a new way the simple petition of Francois Fénelon: "Lord, I know not what I ought to ask of thee; thou only knowest what I need. Teach me to pray. Pray thyself in me. Amen."[2]

As natural and necessary as prayer is to believers, so much of praying remains a God-filled mystery—something He does in and through us (Rom. 8:15-16). Is it God's voice or ours, then, that cries out, "Abba, Father!"? In this book we joyfully answer, "Yes!" It is both!

Our hope is that these written prayers will help you express your own marriage commitment in fresh and meaningful ways while leading you into a deeper love affair with your spouse. And more, that they will encourage you to go ever further in the most important conversation of your life.

DAVID AND HEATHER KOPP

CHAPTER 1

The Power of a Praying Partner

Lord, may we be brought to complete unity in our marriage for our own blessing and, even more, so that everyone we meet will know that You are God—and that You, Jesus, have saved us through love!

A MARRIAGE PRAYER BASED ON JESUS' PRAYER FOR HIS DISCIPLES, JOHN 17:23,26

Sitting in the back, which would be the sixth row of white folding chairs, you look over the other friends and family dressed in their wedding best. You register that the boy in front of you has lifted a whole pocketful of mints. At the piano the last notes of "Jesu, Joy of Man's Desiring" are fading away. The minister is about to begin.

"Dearly beloved, we have come together in the presence of God to witness and bless the joining together of this man and this woman in holy matrimony . . ."

Outside, night has fallen. But in this home, warmed by candlelight and roses and love, two lives are about to become one. If you tip your head just so, you can watch the couple's reflections in the expanse of dark windows in front of you—this man and woman in love, so eager, so nervous, hardly breathing as they listen intently.

"Our Lord Jesus Christ adorned this manner of life by His presence and first miracle at a wedding in Cana of Galilee. It signifies to us the mystery of the union . . ."

You sit back. Memories play in your heart like deep chords. The boy with the mints is counting candles: "fifty-six . . . fifty-seven!"

Soon the bride and groom have exchanged vows. And rings. Then they're kneeling, their faces gone from the window. Now the minister's hands reach wide over two bowed heads as he prays.

3

"Pour out the abundance of Your blessing upon this man and this woman. Defend them from every enemy. Lead them into all peace . . ."

And you gaze past this scene from a marriage, out into that ocean of dark glass ahead of the kneeling lovers. Fifty-seven candles flicker and burn quietly there . . .

A CHERISHED OPPORTUNITY

The story of most weddings unfolds something like ours did—a bride and groom, friends, and family gathered in Christ's presence to seal sacred promises. But whether you were married in a church, on a beach, or at the courthouse, like us you held hands, said "I do," and kissed. Within minutes the ceremony was over.

While our weddings whiz by, our marriages turn into lifelong epics that chronicle the most radical relationship adventure imaginable—"the two shall become one." From the moment we take our vows we know we're part of something holy, mysterious—and hard!

To marry is to become permanently linked with another person's reputation, political views, spiritual life, golf score, and taste in ties. We're no longer two individuals but a couple. As Mike Mason, author of *The Mystery of Marriage*, says, "A marriage is not a joining of two worlds, but an abandoning of two worlds in order that one new one might be formed."[1]

As if the process of becoming one isn't challenging enough, we agree that together we'll face whatever life sends our way—birth and death, sickness, work pressures, raising children, pursuing and often letting go of our most cherished dreams. No wonder the "for better or worse" that sounded so poetic when we wore a rented tux can start to sound impossible.

Those scenes from our wedding ceremony can begin to fade. The candles flicker and sputter . . .

Yet no matter what challenges we face, a cherished opportunity still lies before us. Through prayer we can still receive God's highest blessings and purposes in our marriage. Through prayer we keep the candles lit, nurturing our love relationship. And through prayer, we continue the conversation with Christ that we began on our knees at the altar.

Antoine de Saint-Exupéry wrote, "To love does not mean simply to look at one another but to look together in the same direction."[2] Every time we pray in our marriage, we pick up our vows anew and look steadfastly in the same direction. We say, "I'm still kneeling beside you, Babe. I still love you. And the Lord of the wedding is still present. Let's talk to Him together."

MOTIVATED TO PRAY

Certain needs drive us to our knees repeatedly in marriage:

Because we know life is unsure, we pray for the dreams that drive us as well as for the fears that haunt us. Because we know life is dangerous, we pray for safety and health. Because we know a shared spiritual life will make us stronger, we pray for spiritual unity. And because we know that love is hard work, we pray for laughter and romance.

Any one of these areas of need could make for a lifetime of praying concerns. Taken together, they are part of our God-given urge to protect, care for, and shape the relationship He has given us. But we don't pray just to accomplish. We also pray to grow in wisdom ourselves, to recover, to hold on.

And we pray to worship and to celebrate. "Thank You, Lord, for the way I can talk to my husband!" or "I praise You for the gift of my wife's laughter!"

Often we pray simply because we have to talk. We *long* to talk to the Person who holds together everything we hold dear and who is Himself most dear to us.

And as we pray, regardless of our reason, wonderful things happen that reach far beyond the answers we seek.

"When I know Gary is praying for me, it feels like affection," says Beth, a Minnesota wife and mother of three small children. "It's so meaningful to know that Gary's talking about me to the One who loves me even more than he does! That's better than flowers some days."

Gary feels the benefits of his wife's prayers differently. "If she's joined me in praying about a decision," he says, "then if it goes wrong—if the new car turns out to be a lemon—we can trust God together. As long as we're praying, I can rest assured that it's not up to me alone to make everything work!"

And what if you pray alone, knowing that your partner is *not* praying for you? Special courage is required of spouses who pray alone. In fact, those closet prayers can seem as costly as Mary's vial of perfume lavished on Jesus' feet. But spouses who pray alone find special motivation in Jesus' promise that "Your Father, who sees what is done in secret, will reward you" (Matt. 6:6) and in Paul's reassurances about the amazing sanctifying powers of one believing spouse (1 Cor. 7:14).

Whether we pray alone or together, our prayers express our deepest affections. Our prayers allow us to keep giving our mates, our expectations, and life's heavy load back to God. And our prayers nurture our own spiritual walk. We may start out praying for our mate's safety, but we can't help being touched by God's Spirit as we talk to Him about the one He's given us to love.

THE UPPER ROOM OF MARRIAGE

One of the best prayer lessons for married lovers is to be found up a flight of stairs and behind closed doors where Jesus gathered with His disciples for the Last Supper. We could also call it Jesus' Engagement Dinner. This was the moment when Jesus first announced the new, undying relationship between Himself and His bride-to-be, the church.

We can imagine the room lit by oil lamps, tables spread with savory delights. The years of Christ's public friendship and ministry were over. Something extraordinary was about to happen. "Jesus knew that the time had come," wrote John. "Having loved his own who were in the world, he now showed them the full extent of his love" (John 13:1).

Those hours spent together were filled with reassurances and tender moments. John devoted a quarter of his gospel (chapters 13 through 17) to describing this one evening. After a time of conversation and teaching, Christ concluded with prayer, interceding at length for His bride-to-be (John 17). Jesus' requests for His disciples make a beautiful prayer menu for spouses:

1. For protection and health—"Protect them by the power of your name" (v. 11).

2. For emotional well-being—"I say these things . . . that they may have . . . joy" (v. 13).

3. For purity and integrity—"Sanctify them by the truth" (v. 17).

4. For oneness and harmony—"May they be brought to complete unity" (v. 23).

5. For salvation and spiritual abundance—"Father, I want those you have given me to be with me where I am" (v. 24).

When we pray for our marriage partner in these same ways, we are expressing the kind of love Christ has for each of us. It's this same love Paul had in mind when he wrote, "Husbands, love your wives, just as Christ loved the church and gave himself up for her" (Eph. 5:25).

Paul—confirmed bachelor that he was—called the relationship between Christ and all believers "a profound mystery" (Eph. 5:32). But centuries earlier, the prophet Hosea spoke for God's heart: "'In that day,' says the LORD, '. . . you will call Me "My Husband."' . . . I will betroth you to Me forever; yes, I will betroth you to Me in righteousness and justice, in lovingkindness and mercy; I will betroth you to Me in faithfulness'" (Hos. 2:16,19-20, NKJV).

THE POWER OF A PRAYING PARTNER

The clearest example in the Bible of prayer in a marriage is found in Genesis 25:21: "Isaac prayed to the Lord on behalf of his wife, because she was barren. The Lord answered his prayer, and his wife Rebekah became pregnant." When God answered, He did so in a big way. Rebekah delivered twins, Jacob and Esau.

But, we wonder, is prayer in the context of marriage just another aspect of living out a faithful Christian life? Or do the prayers of husbands or wives for their spouses have special meaning or effectiveness?

The answer seems to be both. But marriage partners who pray draw on some key spiritual principles for blessing:

1. *In marriage we can pray with the power of oneness.* A married couple has become—and will always be in the process of becoming— "one flesh" (Gen. 2:23-24). When we pray as part of this mysterious union, we invite God to accomplish His original purpose to bless and complete us through the relationship.

2. *In marriage we can pray with the power of His presence.* Jesus said He is present in a special way when two or three of His own meet in His name (Matt. 18:20). When we pray and agree together as a couple, we obey Christ's invitation and we experience the "power of three" (see Eccles. 4:12).

3. *In marriage we can pray with the power of insight that comes from intimacy.* No one can pray for us with as much understanding and sincerity as our lifelong partners. When we know and love each other completely, our requests are more likely to be in line with God's purposes. And our thanks for our spouses will flow more naturally (Phil. 1:3-11).

4. *In marriage we can pray with the power of true love.* The effectiveness of every spiritual ministry in the lives of others begins in love; anything else is just a waste of effort, Paul wrote (1 Cor. 13:1-8). When husbands or wives pray in love, they pray with a power that God promises cannot fail.

THE PRAYER OF LOVE

Christian counselor and author Larry Crabb wrote, "Regardless of the circumstances under which people were married, God affords each married partner a unique opportunity to minister in a special way to his or her mate."[3] We may not think of ourselves as ministers as we pray for our spouses, but according to Crabb, if our motives aren't ministry, we're probably only accomplishing manipulation.

When Jesus prayed for His disciples in the upper room, He could have prayed about James's and John's small-minded arrogance, about Peter's flimsy loyalty, or any other of His disciples' failings. But He didn't. He prayed passionately, nonjudgmentally, and lovingly.

In fact, marriage is probably God's favorite workshop for making us more like Jesus. But the chisel work in all this change is God's job, not ours. And that goes for our praying too. "Especially when we're asking God to overcome [another person's] negative qualities, we must be on guard against the sin of a critical, proud spirit cloaked in prayer," write prayer mentors Warren and Ruth Myers. "When we're concerned about a person's negative qualities, it helps to think through to the corresponding positive qualities we hope for, and pray for those. We personally find it easier to have faith *for* the positives than *against* the negatives."[4]

How can we check our motives? One way is to do a love inventory based on Paul's well-known hymn to true love, 1 Corinthians 13:4-8. For example:

The prayer of love is patient: Am I praying with a tolerant, persevering, and realistic attitude (the kind of attitude I need in return on a regular basis)?

The prayer of love is kind: Am I praying with a determination to understand my mate, to listen, to believe the best, to forgive?

The prayer of love is not self-seeking: What's at stake here—my rights, my preferences, my way? Have I resolutely tried to see the big picture and "pray with the mind of Christ"?

The prayer of love is not boastful or proud: In every request for my beloved, do I keep my own ever-present failings in mind? Are my words and tone in prayer genuinely humble?

The prayer of love believes and hopes and endures: Do I pray with all the crazy passion and boundless enthusiasm I felt at our wedding? Do I pray, too, with all the faith and trust that God has been nourishing in me in the years since?

Attitudes make a difference in marital prayers. Without love, all a wife's well-intentioned petitions are just noise (1 Cor. 13:1). Without outward behavior to match an inward attitude of mutual respect and consideration, all a husband's pious requests won't get past the ceiling (1 Pet. 3:7).

SO MANY WAYS TO PRAY

Praying is the sound God's family makes when we are in right relationship with our Lord. The spectrum of that sound includes praise, thanksgiving, confession, petition, intercession, worship—the wonderful hubbub of earnest talking and listening between children and a heavenly Father.

We have tremendous freedom in our praying:

- We can pray anywhere, anytime (Jon. 2:1, 2 Tim. 1:3).
- We can wail out our deepest, least likable feelings and know God will not be shocked or deaf to our pleas (Ps. 102:17, Lam. 2:19).
- We can pray haltingly, simply, confusedly (Rom. 8:26, Ps. 69:33).
- We can pray alone or with other believers (Dan. 6:10, Acts 2:42-47).

- We can pray ecstatically, carried along by God's Spirit, or woodenly, driven by our commitments when all feelings fail us (Eph. 5:18-19, Ps. 102:23-28).
- We can pray silently, wordlessly (Ps. 5:1, Matt. 6:6).
- We can pray over and over for the same request (Luke 18:1-8).

And this book celebrates yet another rewarding freedom in our praying: We can speak Scripture back to God, making it the sincere expression of our own hearts (Col. 3:16).

A GOD WHO ANSWERS

Not only has God given us freedom in our marriages to pray, He has promised that we can be certain our petitions get a response. "Which of you, if his son asks for bread, will give him a stone?" Jesus asked. "If you, then, though you are evil, know how to give good gifts to your children, how much more will your Father in heaven give good gifts to those who ask him!" (Matt. 7:9,11).

Jesus promised that every prayer of a God-seeking person would be answered. "Everyone who asks receives," He said (Matt. 7:8). Always.

But the fact that God always answers doesn't mean that we always get what we want. The answer—which may appear at first to be no answer—might be yes or no, direct or indirect, immediate or deferred. Or the change we at first seek outside of ourselves—"Please help Mike to stop complaining"—may become a prayer for change within—"Lord, teach me how to listen to my husband so he feels genuinely heard."

And sometimes we must simply go forward in faith when God's answers on deeply felt issues remain wrapped in mystery.

Not only has God given us assurances that He hears and answers, He has also given us helps on how to pray in His Word. With the Holy Spirit's aid, we can make them part of an effective prayer experience:

Pray reverently. Keep in mind God's holiness and greatness. Pray with genuine respect and humility (Eccles. 5:1-2, Matt. 6:9).

Pray sincerely. The words don't matter as much as your heart. Bring a deeply felt desire to see God act for your marriage—and a wholehearted willingness to do your part to make those solutions possible (Matt. 6:7-8, Heb. 10:22, Ps. 51:17).

Pray in faith. Simply and completely trust in God's desire for your family's best and in His power to make it happen (Jer. 32:17, Heb. 11:6).

Pray without known sin in your heart or life. Don't let your prayers be hindered by unfinished business with God, your neighbor, or your own family (Prov. 15:8, Mark 12:38-40, 1 John 3:21-22, James 4:8).

Pray according to God's will. Submit your personal desires to God's greater glory and purposes. Test your wishes for your marriage against His revealed truth (1 John 5:14, Matt. 6:10).

Pray in Jesus' name. We have access to the Father through Jesus' name and by His merits. His name is the power above all powers on earth (John 15:16, Eph. 2:18).

Pray thankfully. Recalling God's past goodnesses and His faithful character, surround every new request with thanksgiving and praise (Phil. 4:6, Ps. 22:3).

Pray boldly and persistently. A loving Father is waiting to give you His best, Jesus taught, and it's better than you could ever imagine. Make your requests known, and continue to expect answers (Heb. 4:16, Luke 18:1-8, Acts 12:5).

When we accept God's invitation to a praying ministry in our marriages, we are often surprised to discover how much our own lives change. Not only do we have a very real advantage over the forces that war against our marriages each day, but *we* also benefit. Repeatedly and gently we're reminded of God's loving commitment to us and the relationships we hold dear. We receive the peace and joy He has promised. And we discover new insights into old problems.

On this journey of prayer, we never pray alone. We are actually joining with Christ in His greatest work in heaven today. He, too, stands before the Father interceding for His bride—us (Rom. 8:34). And He gives us His Spirit to help us as we pray (Rom. 8:26-27).

When you think about it, the opportunity to pray for your mate is an amazing invitation from the One who loves him or her most.

Yes, prayer takes patience and discipline, and at times it feels costly. But when we give of ourselves on behalf of our spouses, we always get back more. Frederick Buechner put it this way: "By all the laws of both logic and simple arithmetic, to give yourself away in love to another would seem to mean that you end up with less of yourself left than you had to begin with. But the miracle is that just the reverse is true, logic and arithmetic go hang. To give yourself away in love to somebody else—as a man and a woman give themselves away to each other at a wedding—is to become for the first time yourself fully."[5]

As you pray the prayers in this book, may you feel Jesus take your hand and lead you gently into the center of what might look like scenes from an ordinary marriage—yours. And there may you find love shining, like fifty-seven candles all around.

CHAPTER 2

Why Pray the Bible?

My heart trembles at your word. I rejoice in your promise like one who finds great spoil.

PSALM 119:161-162

P rayer—conversation with God—is so simple that it can be understood and experienced by a five-year-old. And the urge to pray—at least to whisper, "Lord, keep him safe" as your husband drives away—is so basic to living that we can hardly tell where caring ends and praying begins.

So why is it that when we set out to pray consistently and effectively for the one we love most, we find ourselves wondering if we really know how to pray? We become tongue-tied, repetitious, dull. Suddenly we realize how easily our prayers dwindle to worries we breathe half-aloud through the day or mumble as we drift off to sleep at night. *Surely there's more to prayer than this,* we hope. Deep down, we want to pray in a way that makes a difference in us, those we love, and our world. We want to deeply enjoy God's presence, receive His blessings, and be changed into His glorious likeness. We want a prayer life that works.

When we turn to the Bible itself, we find the help we're looking for.

GOD'S PRAYER BOOK

The Bible is a ready-made prayer book for God's family. We "pray the Bible" when we use passages of Scripture to form prayers or when we say the verses directly back to God, making them our own petitions.

Whenever we speak to God with the words of God, we move closer to the kind of vital, effective prayer life we long for.

Several years ago I (David) realized that I'd been praying the Bible all my life—I'd just never called it that before. My first experiences came through my missionary parents. In spite of a speech impediment, my father, Joe Kopp, preached the Word at every opportunity. He used Scripture memorization both to help him overcome his stammer and to teach pre-literate Africans the Bible. Saying Bible passages back to God became part of every village church service as well of our praying at home.

Heather and I have tried to make Scripture prayers a part of our lives together. The opportunities are so varied:

- a prayer of encouragement for a spouse: "Lord, today I claim these wonderful promises from You for my dear wife: 'My kindness, mercies and love for Heather are inexhaustible!'" (from Ps. 52:8, Jer. 31:3);
- a life verse prayed regularly for one of our sons as he moves out on his own: "Lord, I'm confident of this, that You who began a good work in Neil will carry it on to completion" (from Phil. 1:6);
- a screen-saver blessing on the family computer: "The Lord will fulfill his purpose for us. His love for us endures forever—and he never abandons the works of his hands!" (from Ps. 138:8);
- a praise from Scripture written in a secret place on the foundation of our house: "The LORD is good, a refuge in times of trouble. He cares for those who trust in him" (Nah. 1:7).

Praying the Bible is not new theology. Neither is it some kind of magical mumbo jumbo. Yet it is a source of power. Jesus often used

Scripture in His prayers for Himself and His disciples. Throughout the Bible we see examples of godly men and women incorporating God's promises and commands in their petitions to Him. They used the Word in their prayers for encouragement, calling to mind who God is and what He has done. Jesus and His disciples sang the psalms together as part of morning and evening prayers. And at the moment of His greatest agony on the cross, Jesus cried out the words of a psalm: "My God, my God, why have you forsaken me?" (Ps. 22:1).

Many other Bible passages are recorded prayers. Some of the best known are the prayer of Moses after the escape through the Red Sea (Exodus 15); Hannah's song at the temple (1 Samuel 2); Jeremiah's lament over Jerusalem (Lamentations); Jonah's plea for grace (Jonah 2); the song of Mary after the angel's visit (Luke 1:46-55); "The Lord's Prayer" (Matt. 6:9-13); Jesus' prayer for His disciples (John 17:6-19); and Paul's prayers for a young church (Eph. 3:14-21, 6).

Since the time of Christ, Christians throughout the world have used the book of Psalms as an unofficial prayer book for the church. Prayer books designated for public worship contain some of our most enduring examples of Scripture-based prayers. For example, "The Great Thanksgiving," from *The Book of Common Prayer,* is taken from Romans 12:1: "And here we offer and present unto thee, O Lord, ourselves, our souls and bodies, to be a reasonable, holy, and living sacrifice unto thee."[1] The Jesus Movement of the 1970s brought back singing choruses of Scripture as a vibrant part of church worship in many circles.

Praying the Bible for Your Marriage applies this principle to personal prayer. C. S. Lewis, among many others, used written, Bible-based prayers in his devotional life. Lewis said this helped him concentrate, stay doctrinally sound, and know how to pray. Otherwise, he said, "the crisis of the present moment, like the nearest telegraph post, will always loom largest."[2]

THE VOICE THAT CHANGES US

When we pray with the Bible as our guide, we hear God's voice more clearly, and we find creative ways to let God's teachings live in and through us. We can reach farther than letting biblical psalms and prayers speak for us. For example, we can:

- personalize a Bible prayer: "May my spouse and I live together in unity today so that everyone we meet may recognize the power and love of Jesus Christ in us" (a request from the prayer of Jesus for His disciples, John 17:23).
- personalize a Bible verse: "Lord, sometimes I don't know what I'm supposed to ask for or even want. How I thank You that Your Spirit is praying for me right now" (a confession and a thanks from Rom. 8:26).
- personalize a Bible promise, teaching, person, or event: "Lord, teach me self-control. Right now I feel as vulnerable to enemy takeover as a city with broken-down walls" (a request from Prov. 25:28).
- personalize a refrain from Scripture as a response from God: We pray: "You know me completely. Look into my heart and life today; see the brokenness and failure. See the wounds in our marriage, so many of my own making." We hear God answer: "I have seen your ways, but I will heal you; I will guide you and

comfort you. Out of sorrow I will bring praise to your lips" (comfort from Isa. 57:18-19).

Consider some of the benefits of praying Scripture:

Praying the Bible gets us "unstuck." Sometimes we're not diligent in prayer because we have a record of mediocre experiences with it—we get distracted, bored, vague. Mostly we have a hard time getting started. Words and ideas fail us. Praying intentionally with Scripture in mind is like choosing to follow a map into new territory. Suddenly we can spot several worthy destinations. A wife can pray confidently and specifically: "Thank You that as Galen makes You Lord of his future, You *will* show him how to make the right job decision" (Prov. 3:6).

Praying the Bible helps us get our memory back. Sometimes we feel so overwhelmed by feelings and needs that our prayers don't seem to reach beyond the problems. We forget God's character, promises, past faithfulness, goodness, and even His extravagances with us. Praying the truths of the Bible helps us remember what God has done and what He can still do.

Jeremiah was an emotional priest called to speak for God during the siege and fall of Jerusalem. When he focused on the terrors around him, Jeremiah felt personally assaulted, even abandoned by God: "He pierced my heart with arrows from his quiver" (Lam. 3:13). Only when he focused on God's past mercies did he find strength and encouragement: "Yet this I call to mind and therefore I have hope: Because of the LORD's great love we are not consumed, for his compassions never fail" (3:21-22).

Praying the Bible helps us pray more specifically and in line with God's will. Without intending to, we can pray ignorantly, even at cross-purposes with what God wants. Jesus told the Pharisees, "You are in error because you do not know the Scriptures or the power of God" (Matt. 22:29). In the same way we use the Bible to measure the content of a sermon or lesson, we can use Scripture to test our motives and reveal the big picture. When we pray the Bible back to God, we speak to God in the words of God with the truth of God. This encourages us to go beyond, "Lord, help me to treat my wife better," to a more complete expression: "Lord, You ask me to live humbly with my wife, treating her with special tenderness [1 Pet. 3:7]. But my pride keeps me on the defensive, protecting my position or reputation or rights. My pride—a false and exaggerated sense of my own importance—is offensive to You [Prov. 8:13]. I'm truly sorry. Please forgive me."

In this kind of prayer we bring God's revealed will into our thoughts, not just our problem or our wishes for a resolution. And when we pray in line with God's will, He promises to answer (1 John 5:14-15).

Praying the Bible helps us pray with confidence and expectancy. When we know and use Bible truth, we can pray with a more muscular faith. Wayne Spear points out that some Bible promises make God's response so definite that the only sensible expectation on our part is complete confidence. For example, when we pray for the forgiveness of sin, God is committed to one, unfailing response. It's spelled out in 1 John 1:9: "If we confess our sins, he is faithful and just and will forgive us our sins and purify us from all unrighteousness."[3]

Faith is not a belief that "anything can happen," writes Spear, but a confidence that *what God has promised will happen.* [4] When we pray in harmony with the principles of Scripture, we can be sure that our needs will be met even though we leave the how and when to God.

Praying the Bible helps us nurture a growing relationship with God.

Prayer is an ongoing conversation between two very interested parties, and the Bible is the major part of God's recorded end of the conversation. Imagine a young couple who becomes engaged only to be suddenly separated for months by the man's military service. Every day the man sends his fiancée a lengthy letter telling her about his daily activities, describing his hopes and dreams for their future, and declaring the depth of his affection for her. But when the couple finally reunites, his beautiful bride-to-be is completely in the dark about his life, his promises, and plans. Before long they lapse into silence. One day the young woman complains that her suitor never tells her what he's thinking. "I'm not sure how much you really care about me!" she finally exclaims. After some painful probing, the truth comes out: The woman has never actually read her mail. "Usually I just opened the letters to see if you still loved me," she admits. "And, well, then I put them in a safe place . . ."

When we neglect to bring Scripture into our prayer conversation, we can be as confused about who God is as this woman was about her husband-to-be. We struggle needlessly with doubts about God's intentions toward us and our marriage, simply because we haven't read, believed, or remembered His love letter to us.

Praying the Bible can open our hearts to allow the Spirit to minister to us. Scripture leads us into an encounter with the Father-heart of God. We hear our Father's voice: "Fear not, for I have redeemed you; I have summoned you by name; you are mine" (Isa. 43:1). And we bask in His presence. This is the attitude David described in Psalm 131: "I have stilled and quieted my soul; like a weaned child with its mother . . . is my soul within me" (v. 2). Scriptures like this remind us that we are invited to come to God with nothing to give, only with who we are—

listening, surrendering, perhaps broken and in need of comfort or healing. Henri Nouwen described this kind of receptivity as "praying with
open hands," an act of devotion which he said often requires greater
courage but promises a more enduring result.[5]

WHAT PRAYING THE BIBLE DOESN'T MEAN

*Praying the Bible doesn't mean we have to leave out our untidy humanness
when we talk with God.* The Bible leads us toward the truth about our
humanity, not away from it. Consider how many of David's psalms
begin with a cry from the depths of his very human soul. Paul repeatedly asked God to free him from his "thorn in his flesh." Even Jesus
begged God to "take this cup from me." God longs for honest com-
munication with us. Unlike the cashier at the grocery store, when God
asks, "How are you today?" He really wants to know. Of course, we
can't hide our real thoughts and feelings from God anyway. Yet because
we come to God through Christ's righteousness, we approach confidently, sure that God receives us with grace regardless of our faults
(Heb. 10:19-22).

Praying the Bible doesn't mean we pray with magical powers. We pray
"magically" when we believe that a certain arrangement of words, like
the right coins inserted in a vending machine, will guarantee the same
result every time. It's true that we have access to power in Jesus' name,
that we receive power through God's Word, and that we can release
God's power through our faith. But we don't ever leverage God or
control His will, no matter how we pray. Our fallen world comes complete with chaos, tragedy, uncertainty, randomness, and personal trials

of all kinds. Jesus' promise to us is not that we can magically escape them through prayer but that we can overcome them.

Praying the Bible is not about using fancy language or sounding "religious." In Matthew 6, Jesus warned about praying aloud just to look more "spiritual" to others and about bombarding God with excess words in hopes that He will hear us better. We don't need to "talk better" to be acceptable to God, nor can we manipulate or impress Him with our carefully worded prayers.

The true test of our praying lies in our simple faith and a pure devotion to God's will.

MAKING THESE PRAYERS YOUR OWN

In the prayers that follow, you'll find Scripture-based prayers in a variety of formats. References in the text point the way to the Bible passage at hand. The words of the Bible are used as they appear in Scripture or modified slightly for personal application, or the prayer addresses a given passage or collection of verses. Some of the meditations are brief enough to memorize easily or to copy onto paper and slip into a handbag or briefcase.

In an effort to represent the range of concerns husbands and wives share, Heather and I identified eight subject categories: unity and harmony, spiritual intimacy and growth, protection and deliverance, wisdom and guidance, emotional and sexual needs, blessing and provision, thanks and praise, and specific husband and wife concerns.

We encourage you to keep *Praying the Bible for Your Marriage* on your nightstand or on your desk and to use it as part of your daily devotional time. You can also use the index to help you track down a prayer either by title or by topic. We've kept the topical index simple; subjects are arranged under seven felt-need categories like, "Lord, teach us your ways . . . ," or "Lord, help us grow our marriage in/when . . ."

As you spend yourself in prayer on behalf of your marriage, we pray that the Holy Spirit will use this book to encourage you—and that you'll quickly "pass beyond reading into praying."[6]

In Jesus' name we pray—and are confident—that the God who gives endurance, encouragement, and hope [Rom. 15:5,13] will accomplish immeasurably more than all you can ask or imagine because His own power— the same power that raised Jesus from the dead [1 Pet. 1:21]—is at work in you and in the marriage partner you love [Eph. 3:20].

DAILY
PRAYERS

One Plus One

For this reason a man will leave his father and mother and be united to his wife, and the two will become one flesh. So they are no longer two, but one.

MATTHEW 19:5-6

Lord of married lovers,
Only You could defy the law of mathematics to make one plus one equal one. And that "one" is not even two halves that add up to a whole but two drastically different people who add up to an entirely new creation: Us!

We come before You in prayer on behalf of Us—a husband and wife who long to reflect Your beautiful likeness (Gen. 5:1-2) and experience the amazing oneness You promise: "Has not the Lord made them one? In flesh and spirit they are his" (Mal. 2:15).

Yet, You hear the voices, Lord, that attempt to separate Us: "Are you sure you did the right thing?" "You deserve more than this." "What if you get bored?" "Well, as long as you're happy . . ."

But You've shown us "the most excellent way" (1 Cor. 12:31)—cherishing our commitment as we cleave to one another (Gen. 2:24), nurturing mutual respect as we submit to each other (Eph. 5:21), finding our lives as we surrender them to You (Luke 9:24).

And this way of love will never fail (1 Cor. 13:8).

Lord of married lovers, bind us together in an everlasting covenant. We dedicate Us to You.

Amen.

Great Builder

Unless the LORD builds the house, its builders labor in vain.

PSALM 127:1

Lord Jesus,

As we seek to create a marriage and a home together, we come to You, our Great Builder, placing our trust in the plans You have drawn for us. We know Your plans for our marriage are good, to give us hope and an exciting future (Jer. 29:11). If You build our house, we know our foundation is secure, built on solid rock (Ps. 71:3), immovable, unshakable (Ps. 46:1-2).

We trust You to build us walls of security. When the winds of trouble howl, seeking to enter through cracks in the plaster, our hearts will be secure and we will have no fear (Ps. 112:8). Even on stormy days, peace will dwell within our walls (Ps. 122:7).

We ask that Your covering of grace will be the roof of our home (Rom. 6:14). Only when we're living "under grace" can we receive one blessing after another (John 1:16).

And Lord, we ask for lots of windows—the ability to see Your beauty and respond with praise (Psalm 148)—and an open door—the gift of hospitality to strangers as well as friends (Heb. 13:1-2).

Furnish our home with lots of laughter and plenty of joy. May the walls echo with shouts of praise to You, Lord, the great builder of all things that last (Heb. 3:4).

One more thing would make our home complete. We humbly ask You to be our Honored Guest and to dwell with us all the days of our lives (Rev. 3:20).

Amen.

Extract of Pomegranate

*You are a garden locked up, my sister, my bride; you are a spring
enclosed, a sealed fountain. Your plants are an orchard of pomegranates.*

SONGS OF SONGS 4:12-13

Lord of married lovers,
You made the pomegranate red and round and sensual to the touch.
This delicious fruit is the perfect promise of love—seeming to be in
blossom and ripe at the same time. But the pomegranate's clusters of
pleasure are hidden inside a boring, bitter pulp.

Like the pomegranate, the passion in our marriage is sometimes
hard to enjoy because it's wrapped in the pulp of everydayness.

Today we pray that You would give us the commitment to pursue
the passion that can get so buried under layers of household chores,
bills, and daily routines. Forgive us of our tendency to want quick and
easy romance—like settling for fruit juice ready squeezed, preserved in
plastic for $2.99 a liter.

Lord of every holy pleasure, guide our desires and season our expectations. Teach us to seek, to wait, to honor each other, to endure the
mundane, to celebrate the miraculous.

Lord, go with us "early to the vineyards to see if the vines have
budded, if their blossoms have opened, and if the pomegranates are in
bloom"—and there give us heaven's best for lovers today (Song of Songs
7:12).

Amen.

Seasons of Love

There is a time for everything, and a season for every activity under heaven.

ECCLESIASTES 3:1

PRAYING FROM ECCLESIASTES 3:1-12

Lord of time and eternity,
How much we need You in our marriage. Our lives bring so many changes day by day—and we keep changing too.

Help our precious love to endure through every season of marriage. In fact, by Your redeeming love, work each season together for a good that's so good only You can imagine it (Rom. 8:28, Eph. 1:11).

In a time to be born, remind us that You make all things new—including us. You are the Lord of babies and beginnings (Eccles. 3:2).

In a time to die, comfort us in our grief. Help us and those we love to reach in faith for eternity, our real home (vv. 2,11).

In a time to plant, give us seeds of hope. Help us water our relationship with encouragement and perseverance and wait with joy for the good results (v. 2).

In a time to uproot, give us determination to pull up those weeds that are hindering our marriage—old habits, wrong attitudes, false assumptions (v. 2).

In a time to search—for truth or a solution to a nagging problem—give us perseverance (v. 6).

In a time to give up searching, give us grace to be content with things as they are (v. 6).

In a time to be silent, help us to listen with our whole beings to our loved ones (v. 7).

In a time to speak, grant us the wisdom to choose our words carefully and sensitively (v. 7).

In a time to love, help us to give ourselves to each other with glad abandon (v. 8).

In a time to hate—to reject any destroyer of our marriage—help us to respond quickly and decisively (v. 8).

Lord, no matter what kind of season or day we're having, help us to remember that all Your plans for us are good (Jer. 29:11). Thank You that we never walk alone—because of You, we are not just two but a cord of three not easily broken (Eccles. 4:12).

Amen.

Dumb and Dumber

Now a man named Ananias, together with his wife Sapphira, also sold a piece of property. With his wife's full knowledge he kept back part of the money for himself. . . . Peter said to [Sapphira], "How could you agree to test the Spirit of the Lord? Look! The feet of the men who buried your husband are at the door, and they will carry you out also."

ACTS 5:1-2,9

A WIFE'S PRAYER

Lord,

Did Sapphira have her eye on a new dress, or was she simply afraid to question her husband's decision? Either way, I know that by going along with him, she was as guilty of lying to God as he.

Lord, many times I've known my husband and I were making a wrong, selfish, or dishonest choice, but instead of saying, "Stop! Wait! Let's do the right thing," I made us Dumb and Dumber. I sat by and condoned, sometimes even encouraged, our mistakes. And then I excused myself because my husband is "the head" of our home.

Forgive me, Lord! Help me to treasure and defend my integrity, as well as my husband's (Col. 3:9-10). Show me how to be his biggest fan when he makes hard, right choices (1 Pet. 2:19-21). And help me to respectfully point out a better way when he's obviously making a mistake.

Together may we honor You by keeping our commitments and by sharing with others what is ours. Thank You for Your promise that "He [or she] who has clean hands and a pure heart . . . will receive blessing from the LORD and vindication from God his Savior" (Ps. 24:4-5).

Amen.

The Little Man with the Ledger

Make sure that nobody pays back wrong for wrong, but always try to be kind to each other and to everyone else.

1 THESSALONIANS 5:15

A HUSBAND'S PRAYER

Dear Lord Jesus,

There's a shriveled little man in me who grasps a pencil in one hand and a ledger pad in the other. He's the game statistician for our marriage. Most days he scribbles away, never missing a point about our relationship—runs, hits, misses, errors. Especially misses and errors.

[Love] keeps no record of wrongs (1 Cor. 13:5).

I know You're right, Lord. But still I spend hours looking over the little man's shoulders. I memorize and analyze his numbers. I take his scores for the truth.

The truth sets you free. Do not use your freedom to indulge the sinful nature but to serve one another in love (from John 8:32, Gal. 5:13).

O Lord, set me truly free from being so judgmental. Help me to see that the ledger is just a shriveled man's accounting. He's a whiz with numbers but useless with the truth. His calculator is my old nature talking. Show me that what passes for a deep concern about facts and fairness is mostly self-centeredness and pride.

Let mercy be your first concern (Mic. 6:8, CEV).

Yes, Lord! Help me to send Old Prune Face packing today. With Your Spirit's eyes, give me the grace to humbly keep track of every opportunity for kindness instead (Gal. 6:10). In Your name I pray. Amen.

Wonderful Words

My heart is set on keeping your decrees to the very end.

PSALM 119:112

PRAYING FROM PSALM 119

Heavenly Father,

Thank You for the wonderful words You've given us in the Bible. Words of encouragement. Words of guidance. Words of poetry and love and music. Words of judgment and grace. Words that wake us up. Words of life!

All of Your words are God-breathed, full of power, and "useful to teach us what is true and help us do what is right" (from 2 Tim 3:16, TLB).

Today we pray that Your Holy Spirit will open our eyes again to discover the marvelous truths within the words of the Bible (Ps. 119:18). As we try to find a quiet time to hear from You each day, teach us how to follow Your advice in our marriage and in the rest of our lives (v. 33). Give us the kind of spiritual understanding of the Bible that settles deeply in our souls and helps us respond to Your voice (v. 34).

Lord, lead us clearly and firmly in the path of Your teachings (v. 35). Use Your Word to show us what to do in the little and large decisions we encounter in marriage. Give us the wisdom of heaven when life's problems feel beyond us to understand or fix (v. 130).

By applying the powerful, fresh perspective of Your Word, may we steer clear of shortsighted, foolish living (v. 36). Turn our eyes away from wanting what is worthless in the long run (v. 37). Keep renewing our passion for You (v. 40).

Amen.

A Blessing for Light

ay the light of God surround

you today.

May His light shine on your

path for seeing,

in your heart for peace,

and from your face as a gift to others.

FROM PROVERBS 6:23

Something New

Forget the former things; do not dwell on the past. See, I am doing a new thing! Now it springs up; do you not perceive it?

ISAIAH 43:18-19

Lord God,

Sometimes I feel about my marriage like the writer of Ecclesiastes felt about life: "All things are wearisome, more than one can say. . . . What has been will be again, what has been done will be done again; there is nothing new under the sun" (Eccles. 1:8-9).

Whatever our love affair was seems to have faded in the routines of redundant conversations, predictable reactions, lengthening silences.

How my marriage partner and I long for something new today!

Are You doing anything new here, Lord? I know You can. Underneath whatever I can see, You are at work remolding us into Your likeness "with ever-increasing glory" (2 Cor. 3:18). You are the God who can make all things new (Rev. 21:5). We ask for this, Lord.

If I'm in the way of a new thing You are trying to accomplish, please show me. Today I choose to release my partner, my self, and our relationship to change, to becoming different and better. Help us to treat each other with both genuine acceptance *and* great expectations (1 Cor. 13:7). Help us to see and marvel at Your promised miracles springing up everywhere around us, even on this day like every other day.

Amen.

"Charge It!"

Give everyone what you owe him: If you owe taxes, pay taxes; if revenue,
then revenue; if respect, then respect; if honor, then honor.

ROMANS 13:7

Lord,

Sometimes the old Hebrew law sounds pretty good. How wonderful it
would be to send a note to our creditors saying: "Sorry! According to our
religion, seven years are up! We owe you nothing!" (from Deut. 15:1).

Today I pray especially for Your help in the area of debt. We want
to stop giving—to MasterCard! You tell us to let no debt remain out-
standing, except the debt of love (Rom. 13:8). And, "Do not be a man
who . . . puts up security for debts; if you lack the means to pay, your
very bed will be snatched from under you" (Prov. 22:26-27).

We still have our bed, Lord, but we know firsthand how easy it is
to fall into the trap of living beyond our means. Even though it's a way
of life in our society, that's no excuse to toss out Your wise and timeless
commands or to be careless stewards of Your blessings (Matt. 25:14-
30). Debt is a thief! It robs us of both money and opportunities to see
You provide for us in Your own better way.

Forgive us, Lord! Convict and redirect us about those "hidden issues"
in overspending: coveting, selfishness, pride, and lack of faith. Change us
by Your Word today: "Do not love the world or anything in the
world. . . . For everything in the world—the cravings of sinful man, the
lust of his eyes, and the boasting of what he has and does—comes not
from the Father, but from the world. The world and its desires pass away,
but the man who does the will of God lives forever" (1 John 2:15-17).

Amen.

Delilah's Lie

Then she said to him, "How can you say, 'I love you,' when you won't confide in me?" . . . With such nagging she prodded him day after day until he was tired to death.

JUDGES 16:15-16

A WIFE'S PRAYER

Heavenly Father,

The last woman in the Bible I want to identify with is Delilah. Yet I recognize myself in some of her words. How many times have I nagged my husband about something until he wanted to run and hide? Or said to him, "If you loved me, you would . . ."?

Father, I see the shallowness, the self-centeredness behind this manipulation. Delilah's lie is such a powerful one: *If a man loves you, he should give you what you want.* But these motives are so ruinous to a healthy marriage.

Today I pray that You will deliver me from the kind of manipulative behaviors that abuse a love relationship. When I am tempted to use my husband's love for me against him—to be demanding or to pressure him—stop me cold. Remind me that my "win" will be shallow, short-lived, and probably very costly to us both.

Give me strength, Lord, to turn away from Delilah's lie. Show me how to speak "the truth in love" (Eph. 4:15) about my wants and needs, while remembering that "love hurts nobody" (Rom. 13:10, PH).

Amen.

Listen to Her Hunches

While Pilate was sitting on the judge's seat, his wife sent him this message: "Don't have anything to do with that innocent man, for I have suffered a great deal today in a dream because of him."

MATTHEW 27:19

A HUSBAND'S PRAYER

Lord of creation,

When You took woman from the side of man, it seems You forgot that man had no parts to spare. Or maybe You intended to leave us males— fine specimens that we are—forever missing circuits, now and then fuzzy-screened, sometimes going quite blank.

Lord of creation, You seem to have left me with a bone-memory of that previous existence—before You said, "It is not good for the man to be alone" (Gen. 2:18). Maybe that memory is what tricks me into making neanderthal claims like, "I'm doing just fine on my own, thanks." But it's not so. Some parts of me are missing . . .

Thank You for the beautiful woman who miraculously completes my humanness—my wife, my help-meet. She is my other, better half. Her name is "Flesh of my flesh" (Gen. 2:23). She is Your best earthly gift to me. Help me learn from her today and live more completely through her. Wake me up to really see and receive my Eve—to accept and understand that my wife knows some things I don't.

Teach me from Your Word today:

—Elkanah must have been taken aback when his wife explained her rash vow to give God their firstborn son. But he trusted her and supported her spiritual impulse. Along with her, he released their little boy, Samuel, into temple service. And You, Lord, raised up for Yourself a faithful priest who changed the course of Jewish history (1 Samuel 1-3).

—David in the heat of anger allowed himself to be slowed down and finally persuaded by the "intelligent and beautiful" Abigail, his wife-to-be. At a time when his whole life seemed like a nightmare, David heard Abigail remind him of who "the real David" was and why he should still believe in his future (1 Samuel 25).

—Young Jesus didn't go with His first inclination at the wedding in Cana. Instead He trusted His mother's insight. Mary seemed to know something that even the virgin-born Carpenter didn't: The time had finally come for Him to do a miracle (John 2:1-11)!

—But Pilate didn't listen to his wife. He thought her hunches weren't logical or good for his career. And afterward, all the water in Jerusalem couldn't wash the innocent Messiah's blood from Pilate's hands (Matt. 27:19-26).

Lord, complete me through my wife today. Help me to put aside all pride and stubbornness that might keep her from becoming the "flesh of my flesh." By Your provision, my marriage is Your mysterious new plan for me to be the "complete male." Help me to listen to her hunches.

Amen.

Rise and Shine

Wake up, O sleeper, rise from the dead, and Christ will shine on you.

A MEDITATION PRAYER TO START THE DAY

In the morning, O Lord,
You hear our voice.
In the morning
we lay our requests before You
and wait in expectation.
This is the day You have made, Lord!
We will rejoice
and be glad in it!

FROM PSALM 5:3, 118:24

Cat Fights

If you keep on biting and devouring each other, watch out or you will be destroyed by each other.

GALATIANS 5:15

Lord,

We come to You, God of peace (Heb. 13:20), and humbly ask that Your peace would rule in our hearts (Col. 3:15). You know about those times when my mate and I sound like cats fighting outside the window at night. The problem isn't that we disagree but that we attack each other instead of the problem (yet how much we do love each other, Lord!).

Your Word reminds us that most arguments start from selfish desires (James 4:1). We want what we want, we want it our way, and we want it now! What silly arrogance! We are both humiliated by our behavior, Lord.

Today we ask You to save us from our need to be right, our determination to win, our tendency to punish. We want to forgive each other as freely as You forgive us (Col. 3:13)—even when we haven't received the kind of affirmation, understanding, or apology we think we deserve.

We hold this picture of peace in our minds today: "How good and pleasant it is when a man and wife live together in unity. It is like precious oil poured on the head, running down on the beard, running down on Aaron's beard, down upon the collar of his robes" (from Ps. 133:1-2).

Yes, Lord, may the oil of Your peace anoint us beautifully today. Amen.

Smiling

hat counts is not what we do, not the amount of things we do, but the love we put into our actions, since those actions are our love for God in action.

Some visitors to Calcutta asked me to tell them something that would be useful for them to lead their lives in a more profitable way. I answered, "Smile at each other. Smile at your wives, at your husbands, at your children, at all, without looking at the one at whom you are smiling. Let mutual love for others grow each day in all of you." At this point one of them asked me, "Are you married?"

I answered, "Yes, I am married to Jesus. And sometimes it is difficult for me to smile at him because he is too demanding."

It is true: sometimes Jesus can ask too much of you. But it is in such moments that our smile becomes more beautiful.

MOTHER TERESA

Gentle Comfort

A happy heart makes the face cheerful, but heartache crushes the spirit.

PROVERBS 15:13

Lord,

I know You understand the heartache my mate is experiencing right now. How I thank You, loving Lord of our marriage, that You feel our heartaches even more than we do!

Today I pray that You will especially ease my mate's suffering about _____. Show me how to be Your hands and feet, giving an encouraging word or a gentle touch at just the right moment.

You are a God of compassion who understands what we humans experience in suffering and temptation (Heb. 4:15). In fact, You carried all our sorrows on Your shoulders when You died for us (Isa. 53:3-4).

Give me the kind of wise insight, Lord, that comes only from You (James 1:5). Help me be a healer, bringing cheer with my own optimism and strong words of hope (Prov. 15:30). Above all, let me receive Your comfort so that I can comfort the one I love with the wonderful comfort You give me (2 Cor. 1:3-4).

By Your Spirit, turn these hard times of heartache into opportunities for us to learn this wonderful promise: "Be of good courage, and he shall strengthen your heart" (Ps. 31:24, KJV).

In Your name I pray.

Amen.

In the Company of Sinners

But go and learn what this means: "I desire mercy, not sacrifice." For I have not come to call the righteous, but sinners.

Jesus, lover of sinners,

Today we are filled with gratefulness for Your love! We are among those sinners who desperately needed saving, Lord. And You saved us! That's why we want our marriage to be an example of Your mercy on the least lovable and most sinful among us.

Deliver us, Jesus, from the impulse to be disdainful and rejecting toward those who are living an openly immoral lifestyle. We remember how You defended an adulterous woman who was dragged before You by a condemning crowd: "If any one of you is without sin, let him be the first to throw a stone at her" (John 8:7).

Deliver us, Jesus, from our arrogant tendency to shun those who want to love You but are captives of addictions and destructive choices. We remember Your words to the prostitute who anointed Your feet with perfume: "Her many sins have been forgiven—for she loved much" (Luke 7:47).

Deliver us, Jesus, from our selfish desire to socialize only with those who already know You. We remember how You dined in the homes of people with terrible reputations. When a seeker came to You under cover of darkness, You told him: "God did not send his Son into the world to condemn the world, but to save the world through him" (John 3:17).

Right now, dear Lord, we repent of those times when we have

excelled at being "religious" but failed to show mercy and love to those who were most in need of it.

This is what You require, Lord:

Mercy. Not religion.

Mercy. Not quick judgment.

Mercy. Not convenient diagnosis.

Mercy. Not social superiority.

Mercy!

Today, Jesus, when we meet the sinful, the lost, the sick, the skeptical, the angry, the obnoxious, the proud, the rich, the criminal, the weak—help us take to heart Your living and dying request: "Be merciful, just as your father is merciful" (Luke 6:36, 23:34).

Amen.

Lover's To-Do List

Do not merely listen to the word, and so deceive yourselves. Do what it says.

JAMES 1:22

Dear Lord Jesus,

In marriage it's so convenient to mistake intention for accomplishment; it's easy to say "love" but so hard to do it. Lord Jesus, please be our teacher—You perfectly lived out love in both word and deed. Please lead us forward today in the simple, hard wisdom that James writes about.

If we promised each other to love "till death do us part," why is it so hard to get up with the baby when it's the other person's turn? If we promised before many witnesses to love "for better or worse," why can't we try harder to honor each other in front of others?

Teach us, Rabbi. Change us, Redeemer. We want to keep investing genuine love in our marriage, to love not merely in theory or in words but in sincerity and in practice (1 John 3:18, PH).

Help me to keep a practical "Lover's To-Do List" today: finishing something I have promised to do, pitching in on a least-favorite chore, displaying a cheerful willingness to get up from my comfortable chair. And when simple words of affection *are* the toughest thing to do, give me a ready tongue.

Graciously give me Your strength to act when I am tired or unmotivated (Phil. 2:13). When I forget everything else, help me to remember Your kingdom-secret for two people living together: "In everything, do to others what you would have them do to you" (Matt. 7:12).

Amen.

Father, Father!

And when you pray, do not keep on babbling like pagans, for they think they will be heard because of their many words.

O heavenly Father,
Thank You that Jesus showed us and taught us how to pray to You! Your Son told us this about You, Father: You wait eagerly to hear from us and to answer generously (Matt. 7:7, John 16:23). Thank You!

Hear the words and meditations of this husband and wife:

Our Father in heaven. Yes, Lord God, You are our Father, the source of this family's identity, provision, and sense of belonging. And You exist so completely above and apart from us, You are so *other*—yet You are still "Daddy" (Rom. 8:15).

Hallowed be Your name. We come to You with reverence today. Incredibly, we stand before You white and pure—welcome in Your presence by the holy covering of Christ, the precious gift that makes communion with You possible (Isa. 61:10, 1 Cor. 1:30). Your name, Father, will be on our lips today—whispered, sung, worshiped, defended.

Your kingdom come, Your will be done on earth as in heaven. Be Most High King in our marriage today. In big life matters, show us Your every wish and requirement (Ps. 119:33-35). And in small daily things, be Master too—of our jokes, our disagreements, our compliments, our lovemaking, our daydreams. May Your kingdom principles be lived out in our marriage each moment.

Give us today our daily bread. Yes, Lord! It's not the company or the bank or the national economy that gives us what we need to survive. It's You. That's why we breathe Your name gratefully over everything from oatmeal to sautéed shrimp. Without Your gifts, we'd starve (Luke 1:53).

Forgive us our debts, as we also have forgiven our debtors. O Father, all our best efforts are just rags that You somehow transform and redeem (Isa. 64:6, Ps. 130:7). So do Your miracle, God! Wash away the sins that cling to us like pitch. And lead us by Your Spirit into that milk-white grace of forgiving others.

And lead us not into temptation, but deliver us from the evil one. Save us from dangerous, "perfectly sensible" decisions, Lord. Save us from obviously stupid indulgences and errors. And wake us up to Satan's deadly devices—they dangle and glitter everywhere in sight. Since that apple in the garden, Lord, we're all dizzy from snakebite. Save us!

For thine is the kingdom and power and glory forever. You are Lord of our marriage. You are Most High King *and* Daddy. You are hope and life to us today. May all power and worship, all ownership and right, all credit and honor be Yours, heavenly Father.

I _____ , husband, and I _____ , wife, pray to You in the love of Your Son, Jesus Christ, who taught us to pray.

Amen.

Make Us Stars

Do everything without complaining or arguing, so that you may become blameless and pure, children of God without fault in a crooked and depraved generation, in which you shine like stars in the universe as you hold out the word of life.

Blessed Morning Star,

Today this is our prayer! Make us stars—not the kind who win recording contracts, fame, and fortune—but the kind who reflect Your glory. We want our marriage to be a glowing proof of Your love, Lord!

May our marriage stand out in this dark generation because we encourage others to experience new life in Christ. For "those who are wise will shine like the brightness of the heavens, and those who lead many to righteousness, like the stars for ever and ever" (Dan. 12:3).

May our marriage stand out in this dark generation because we try daily to treat each other in ways that please You, "for the fruit of the light consists in all goodness, righteousness and truth" (Eph. 5:9).

May our marriage stand out in this dark generation because we don't support or befriend those who oppose You, "for what do righteousness and wickedness have in common? Or what fellowship can light have with darkness?" (2 Cor. 6:14).

Finally, Lord, may our marriage stand out in this dark generation because we genuinely love others. "Whoever loves his brother lives in the light, and there is nothing in him to make him stumble" (1 John 2:10).

In all these ways, Morning Star, may our marriage shine for You! Amen.

Love Stories

The LORD, the God of heaven . . . will send his angel before you so that you can get a wife for my son from there.

GENESIS 24:7

O *"Matchmaker of Heaven,"*
What a delight to call You by the name of Matchmaker, Lord God! You care about crushes and first loves and soul mates. You send Your angels to bring a man and a woman together—as You did for a lonely Isaac and a distant Rebekah. You work through wise mothers-in-law—as You did through Naomi for the dutiful young widow Ruth (Ruth 2–4).

Truly, how sweet is the love You have lavished on us (1 John 3:1).

Matchmaker, we see clues of Your affection and involvement in so many of the love stories You told us in Your Word. In the faithful devotion of Elkanah for his barren wife, Hannah (1 Samuel 1–2). In the sacrificial forgiveness of Hosea for his wandering Gomer (Hosea 3). In the brave loyalty of beautiful, young Esther for brash King Xerxes (Esther 5).

And yet, Matchmaker, we also hear Your voice from the wings even when Your love stories seem to falter.

—When everything on the stage of love is a mess: "Then David comforted his wife Bathsheba, and he went to her and lay with her" (2 Sam. 12:24).

—When believing in love requires extraordinary faith: "Joseph . . . did what the angel of the Lord had commanded and took Mary home as his wife" (Matt. 1:24).

And yes, Lord, even when a match "made in heaven" is tested by deep differences: "Isaac, who had a taste for wild game, loved Esau, but Rebekah loved Jacob" (Gen. 25:28).

Thank You, Lord, that we don't have to be "made for each other" to be *meant* for each other! Thank You, Lord, that You are not only a matchmaker, You are a marriage maker! Regardless of how we come together, as soon as we marry, You become our "witness"—and the champion of our union (Mal. 2:14). Now we belong to You (v. 15).

Today we rest in the sweet knowledge that our love story is precious in Your eyes. And we pray that You will continue to make us into a match that will proclaim Your glory.

Amen.

Company's Coming

Offer hospitality to one another without grumbling.

1 PETER 4:9

Lord,
Today we pray that You would create a desire in both of us to be truly hospitable. The word *hospitality* sounds so pretty, but it's not always easy to carry off. It's always easier to entertain friends we know well, but we also want to be prepared to "entertain strangers" (Heb. 13:2).

Lord, make us like Gaius, the Roman Christian about whom almost nothing is written *except* that the whole church in Rome enjoyed his hospitality (Rom. 16:23). (But could we have a bigger house?)

When people visit us, help us not to get hung up on whether our dishes match or our kids' rooms are clean. Instead, make us spiritually sensitive to what our guests might feel or need. Help us to ask good questions, to listen well, to take time, and to truly care about their lives (Phil. 2:4).

Lord, what can we do right now? What person do You want us to bless in this way?

Let this be a day when company's coming.

Amen.

My Maker, My Husband

For your Maker is your husband—the LORD Almighty is his name—the Holy One of Israel is your Redeemer; he is called the God of all the earth.

ISAIAH 54:5

Lord and Maker,

How amazing to me that You, my Redeemer, are indeed a "husband" to me! You love me even more than my earthly husband, and my relationship with You is of even greater importance and promise than my marriage.

Thank You for Your patience with me when I expect my husband to meet spiritual and emotional needs that only You can meet, Lord. Some days I act like Rachel when she demanded a baby from Jacob. And my poor husband feels like Jacob felt when he protested, "Am I in the place of God?" (Gen. 30:2).

Today I praise You for giving me a husband of flesh and blood. But I also want to know what it means to have You for my heavenly husband. You are ready to meet my deepest needs (Ps. 116:6), You lavish on me great affection (1 John 3:1), You champion me before the evil one (1 John 2:1), and You comfort me when I'm distressed (2 Cor. 1:4). How grateful I am! I want to love You deeply and faithfully in return.

Lord, when life gets ordinary and my husband turns out to be only human, may I hear You whispering in my ear, "Return, . . . for I am your husband" (Jer. 3:14). Yes, I will cherish Your vow to me: " 'With everlasting kindness I will have compassion on you,' says the LORD your Redeemer" (Isa. 54:8).

Amen.

Prayer from the Dust

I am laid low in the dust; preserve my life according to your word.

Dear Lord of my marriage,

I long to be more like You today. But this is where I start from—dust. Only You can renew me inside and out (Ps. 119:25,40).

And that's my prayer for today. By a miracle I don't understand, shape me—yes, remake me daily—in mind, body, spirit, and heart to please and serve You. I don't want any other influence or power to determine the direction or value of my life (Rom. 12:1-2).

Is there an area, especially in marriage, that Your Spirit is speaking to me about? What is it, Lord? I listen to You now.

Pursue my mate and me, Lord. Don't let us get away—into laziness, mediocrity, self-centered routines, unredeemed attitudes and assumptions. When we slip or stray, chase us! Seize us! Shape us! We are all Yours (John 17:9)!

Receive our praise from the dust today: We praise You because You are an awesome God (Ps. 47:2). We trust You completely because every single one of Your intentions for us is awesome (Jer. 29:11). We worship You because only You have the power to make us new beings (2 Cor. 5:17).

Yes, keep on doing what only You can do—changing all of us into Your beautiful likeness (2 Cor. 3:18).

Amen.

A Very Dangerous Business

Prayer is, after all, a very dangerous business. For all the benefits it offers of growing closer to God, it carries with it one great element of risk: the possibility of change.

In prayer we open ourselves to the chance that God will do something with us that we had not intended. . . . This possibility excites us, but at the same time there is a fluttering in the stomach that goes with any dangerous adventure.

EMILIE GRIFFIN

The Little That Is More

Better a meal of vegetables where there is love than a fattened calf with hatred.

PROVERBS 15:17

Gracious Lord,

We're such hungry animals—always wanting something more or different, always striving. Is this part of the old, unchanged nature that wars with Your Spirit?

Your Word to us for today is about the veggies-with-love that are a feast. Forgive us for our nagging discontent. Turn us around when we go chasing after the "fattened calf"—even at the expense of family harmony (James 4:2). Teach us by Your Spirit that "godliness with contentment is great gain. If we have food and clothing—and love!—we will be content with that" (from 1 Tim. 6:6-9).

We already know from experience that happiness never comes from more stuff in our homes anyway (Luke 12:15) but from more life in our hearts (John 10:10). Let us be restless only for more of You!

Thank You, Father, that we do have love. Yes, even on macaroni-and-cheese weeks, we are blessed and rich.

Amen.

For Better or Worse

*So the LORD God banished him from the Garden of Eden to work the
ground from which he had been taken.*

GENESIS 3:23

Heavenly Father,
How quickly the easy bliss of those first lovers in Eden turned into
bitter trials. Love that had been innocent, safe, and effortless suddenly
required commitment, forgiveness, and hard work.

As far as we know, You didn't ask Adam and Eve to exchange marriage vows (Gen. 2:22-25). But theirs was the ultimate example of enduring both good times and bad. They shared love first in a perfect
Eden and afterward in a difficult exile (Gen. 3:23).

Hear our own "after Eden" marriage prayer today: We want to be
faithful to the vows we made—to love each other "for better or worse,
for richer or for poorer, in sickness and in health."

We know that each of our vows will be tested by life—that marriage doesn't let us escape the consequences of our fallen world. In fact,
Your Word tells us, "He who finds a wife finds what is good" (Prov.
18:22), but it also says, "Those who marry will face many troubles in
this life" (1 Cor. 7:28). Lord, we accept the reality of both—the better
and the worse.

And Lord, how wonderful are those "better" times—when we
glimpse Eden in our romance and in the passionate wonders of sexual
love. Yes, we happily praise You for the times when we are healthy, getting along well, and richly blessed!

But today show us also the hidden opportunities in those painful, "worse" times—when conflicts, sickness, and financial pressures weigh heavily upon us. It is harder to feel grateful for these things. But we know You use weaknesses and trials to test and strengthen us and our marriage (James 1:2-4).

And this is truly what we desire, Lord! We want to learn to love at all times (Prov. 17:17). We want a relationship that is full of kindness, patience, faith, and hope. We want a love that will never fail (1 Cor. 13:4-8).

Right now, we stand in Your presence to embrace once more those sacred marriage vows. Yes, Lord, today we choose each other all over again—for better or worse.

We praise and thank You, God of love before and after Eden.

Amen.

We're Convinced!

No, in all these things we are more than conquerors through him who loved us.

ROMANS 8:37

PRAYING FROM ROMANS 8:38-39

Lord,

Every day someone fails to convince us of something—our kids, that they really did clean their rooms; the salesman who calls during dinner, that we really do need another credit card.

We're skeptics, Lord. But today we choose to be joyfully, thoroughly, and irrevocably *convinced* about the one thing that matters most: Your love!

For we are convinced that neither death nor life,
(not cancer, accidents, handicaps, or random crimes)
neither angels nor demons,
(not cults, spiritual oppression, evil in media, or crazed psychopaths)
neither the present nor the future,
(not any crisis looming now or any tragedy yet to come)
nor any powers,
(not political, financial, military, cultural—even the IRS)
neither height nor depth,
(not success, wealth, and achievement, or failure, poverty, and loss)
nor anything else in all creation,
(not the ozone, auto repairmen, hurricanes, even untrained puppies)
will be able to separate us from the love of God
that is in Christ Jesus our Lord!
Amen!

Book of Sorrows

You became sorrowful as God intended. . . . Godly sorrow brings
repentance that leads to salvation and leaves no regret.

2 C O R I N T H I A N S   7 : 9 - 1 0

A H U S B A N D ' S P R A Y E R

Heavenly Father,
Today I acknowledge before You my book of sorrows—the record of
the ongoing failures and mistakes in my marriage that I've been trying
to hide from myself and from You. But You see everything, Father
(Prov. 15:3).

I am Your son. Hear my confession:

You ask me to live humbly with my wife, treating her with special
tenderness (1 Pet. 3:7). But my pride keeps me on the defensive, protecting my position or reputation or rights. My pride—a false and exaggerated sense of my own importance—is offensive to You (Prov. 8:13).
And it's a continual source of injury to my wife. I'm truly sorry and
humbly repent. Please forgive me, Lord.

You ask me to put my wife's needs first (Phil. 2:3-4). But more often, my love for my wife starts from my own needs. My respect for her
starts with my appreciation for what she brings to my life and for my
own admirable skill in choosing her. My patience with her is too often
rooted in the hope of getting something I want, like peace, concession,
or praise. I'm truly sorry and humbly repent. Please forgive me, Lord.

You ask me to love my wife like my own body (Eph. 5:28). But
while I watch out for myself reflexively, I have to keep notes in my

Day-Timer to pay her little attentions. I consider my physical needs her business but not often the other way around. What I really want is for her beauty and her body to take care of my lusts and passions enough that I won't be distracted by any other woman, real or imaginary. I'm truly sorry and humbly repent. Please forgive me, Lord.

You ask me to be of one heart and one spirit with my wife (Phil. 2:2). But instead, I treat her like Your contribution to my success, my personal assistant to help me realize the dreams You have implanted in me. How much time do I spend losing myself and my wishes in making her dreams come true? I hardly know what they are. I'm truly sorry and humbly repent. Please forgive me, Lord.

You ask me to bear with my wife's faults and weaknesses in love (Col. 3:13). You promise that even our faults are part of Your plan for refining us (1 Cor. 11:32). But I keep trying to fix my wife's faults, keeping track of how many ways I'm inconvenienced by them. Meanwhile, I expect her not to walk out of the room when I get angry and loud. I'm truly sorry and humbly repent. Please forgive me, Lord.

You ask me to love deeply and with sincerity (1 Pet. 1:22). But I listen to her with practiced gestures of attention and concern. I tell her I understand, but I'm not sure if I do—or if I want to work that hard. And yet, I expect her to listen to my ramblings, diatribes, and worryings with rapt attention. I'm truly sorry, and I humbly repent, Lord.

Today, hear my confession. Take away the sin that separates me from You and from my wife (Eph. 2:14). Let Your Word penetrate to those inner places of soul, intention, spirit, habit, denial, numbness, prideful resistance (Heb. 4:12). For my wife's sake, make me a new man in Christ (2 Cor. 5:17). I humbly ask these things in Your name, Father.

Amen.

A Worker's Prayer

Whatever you do, work at it with all your heart, as working for the Lord, not for men.

My heavenly Father,

I pray today for a worthy "work attitude." I'm asking as one who wants to be diligent but sometimes has trouble "getting up out of the easy chair" for my marriage.

It's Satan's lie that good things happen without effort. But Your Word warns that laziness in any arena only leads to poverty, dissatisfaction, and disgrace (Prov. 10:4, 13:4, 28:19). Please grow in me a passion to be a worker in my home—one who gets things done, who sees a need and *acts,* who doesn't just sit back and expect to enjoy a good life because my partner is working hard (2 Thess. 3:10).

Help me today to reach for tasks enthusiastically—and without complaining (Phil. 2:14). In fact, the more menial or unnoticed the work, the more I want to carry it out as a gift to You, my God (Col. 3:23).

May my diligent efforts honor You and bless others around me:

—like faithful Noah who worked for years to build an ark for his family when no flood was in sight (Genesis 6, Heb. 11:7).

—like humble Ruth who gleaned day after day so her mother-in-law could be provided for (Ruth 2).

—like passionate Jacob who herded sheep for fourteen years so he could earn the right to marry Rachel (Genesis 29).

Every day, O Lord, "establish the work of our hands for us—yes, establish the work of hands" (Ps. 90:17).

Amen.

Sifted by Satan

Simon, Simon, Satan has asked to sift you as wheat. But I have prayed for you, Simon, that your faith may not fail. And when you have turned back, strengthen your brothers.

LUKE 22:31

Lord,

This verse always makes me nervous. What if Satan has asked to sift me or my marriage?

And then I remember Your wonderful encouragement to Peter— "Because I'm praying for you, I know you'll make it through. In fact, to show you how sure I am, here's what to do once you've overcome."

Today I pray that when our marriage is tested by Satan—or simply by hard times—that we will cling to Your promises, Your people, Your record of goodness.

Thank You that You are always praying for us (Rom. 8:34). Thank You that You love us passionately, know us intimately, and protect us completely from anything we can't handle (1 Cor. 10:13).

See us through those times of trial, Lord. We are just as capable of betraying You as Peter was. But we don't want to! What a blessing it is to know that if we do fail You, You still won't fail us. Even if we're faithless, You'll still be faithful (2 Tim. 2:13).

Like You did with Peter, Lord, bring us back to You. Let us catch sight of You on the beach of our lives just when we think all is lost (John 21). And after Satan has done his best to sift us, we will tell You again: "We love You, Lord! Yes, we really do!"

Amen.

Crazy Love

Now that you have purified yourselves by obeying the truth so that you have sincere love for your brothers, love one another deeply, from the heart.

1 PETER 1:22

Lord,

Sometimes the hardest person to love is the one I'm committed to loving the most. But You ask us to love one another at all times (Prov. 17:17), deeply and sincerely (1 Pet. 1:22), and even when the other person doesn't love us in return (Luke 6:27,32).

That's crazy love, Lord—but it's also the only sane way to make a marriage work. Show my spouse and me today how to love each other in the same radical way You love us—freely (Matt. 10:8), completely (Mark 12:31), and even extravagantly (John 13:1).

We can't do this alone. By Your love working in us, help us to love when we can't figure out what to make for dinner, when we mix our signals and keep each other waiting, when we are both too tired to get up and let the dog out.

O Lord, help us to love not just in words—"Yes, Honey, of course I love you"—but in sincere, even costly ways that really communicate affection and care to our beloved (1 John 3:18).

Today I choose to love my dear mate with the same crazy, unconditional love that You lavished on all of us when You sent Your own perfect Son to die so that we could live with You forever (John 3:16).

Amen.

How Could Anything Be Said . . . ?

ow could anything rightly be said about love if You were forgotten,

O God of love, from whom all love comes in

heaven and on earth;

You who held nothing back but gave every-

thing in love;

You who are love, so the lover is only what

he is through being in You?

SOREN KIERKEGAARD

Unequally Yoked

*For the unbelieving husband has been sanctified through his wife,
and the unbelieving wife has been sanctified through her believing
husband.*

1 CORINTHIANS 7:14

A PRAYER FOR AN UNSAVED SPOUSE

All-knowing Lord,
The one I love so dearly doesn't know You! Sometimes this unequal
yoking seems more than I can bear. It's lonely, Lord. There's a chasm
between us that feels impossible to bridge.

How I long for us to pray and worship as one, to raise our family
united in You. How I yearn for the assurance that I'll see my beloved in
eternity. I grieve when I think, "What if?"

You have said You don't want anyone to perish (2 Pet. 3:9). You
know those who are Yours (2 Tim. 2:19). But it's only in *Your* time,
Your way, for *Your* glory that Your people come to You.

So, I wait. (But the waiting's so hard!)

In the meantime, Lord, help me not to focus on the chasm between me and my spouse but on all those sacred commitments that
bind us together. Help me to be an instrument of Your grace and peace
(1 Pet. 1:2).

And may I love—truly love—the one You've given me, remembering always that You're the one who sets the lonely in families (Ps. 68:6)
and that in some mysterious way You have already "sanctified" my partner through my faith in You (1 Cor. 7:14).

I look to You, today and tomorrow, for comfort in times of loneliness, for strength to endure times of misunderstanding, and for grace to be Your living witness in my marriage for better, for worse, forever.

Amen.

He Is Yours

How precious to me are your thoughts, O God!

PSALM 139:17

PRAYING FROM PSALM 139 (A WIFE'S PRAYER)

Lord,

Some days I feel like I don't understand my husband. What is he thinking? How does he really feel about me? What do "Uh-huh" and "Fine" really mean? Because I love him so much, I wish I could see deep inside his heart and mind.

Today, help me remember that *You* know him completely. You love him much more than I ever will—You are his truest lover. Your thoughts are always about him—yes, how precious to this wife are Your thoughts, O God!

Thank You that I don't have to search him out completely, because You've already explored every corner of his being, his thoughts, and his actions (vv. 1-2). And You are lovingly at work, bringing him to a fuller spiritual understanding every day (Ps. 42:8).

Thank You that I don't have to know where my husband is every moment—physically or emotionally. You are familiar with all his ways (Ps. 139:3). Your constant presence is a guaranteed blessing (Acts 17:27).

Thank You that I don't have to pry words out of my husband or get frustrated when he doesn't seem to want to talk. You know every thought before it comes out of his mouth—even if it never does (Ps. 139:4)! Your Spirit and Your Word are invading and redeeming his innermost thoughts and desires every day, quite apart from my mis-guided attempts (vv. 23-24).

Thank You that I don't have to be obsessed about my husband's safety, his success, or his choices. You go behind him and before him to show him the way and to protect him at every moment. You place Your hand of blessing on his head (v. 5, TLB). You are the God of his life—I don't need to try to play the part.

When I remember that there's nowhere in the world that either my husband or I can go to escape Your presence (v. 7), it's easier to accept the limitations of my own love. To simply let go. To humbly ask for wisdom to know how to lovingly and creatively invite my husband into intimacy, never require or manipulate it.

Today I will meditate on Your thoughts toward my husband. Thank You, Lord, for Your amazing love for him. Thank You for Your perfect intentions for his life. And for mine.

Amen.

Praises for Kisses

Your lips are like a scarlet ribbon; your mouth is lovely. . . . How
beautiful you are and how pleasing, O love, with your delights!

SONG OF SONGS 4:3, 7:6

A HUSBAND'S PRAYER

Dear Lord God,

Thank You today for the pleasures of married love. Thank You for
physical gifts of kisses, of smooth skin, of soft eyelashes, of my wife's
lovely voice in my ear. Thank You for the wonders of sexual desire and
expression and release.

Thank You, God of Spirit, that You gave husbands the gift of
senses—and all the nerve endings and hormones and imagination to
enjoy them (Ps. 139:14).

Thank You, God of marriage, that You put it in a woman's heart
from the beginning to want to please her husband (Gen. 3:16).

Thank You, God of love, that You consider the physical and emotional attraction between a man and a woman one of the wonders of
Your created world (Prov. 30:18-19).

Thank You, God of romance, that You put a whole book in the
Bible to celebrate beautiful bodies, pounding hearts, and the swoony,
sweet flirtations of a love-struck man and woman (Song of Songs).

Thank You, God of faithful wedded bliss, that my wife can satisfy
my sexual needs for my whole life, not just until we hit a seven-year
itch or a midlife crisis (Prov. 5:18-19).

Thank You, God of holy passions, that even single-minded, celibate

Paul taught that a man and wife should protect and express their sexual enjoyment of each other (1 Cor. 7:5).

And thank You, God of married lovers, for the way my wife leaves a fragrance on her pillow and a confidence in my heart all day that being in my arms is about her favorite place on earth (Song of Songs 1:3, 8:3).

In our holy dance of the senses today, may I bring delight to my wife and honor to You.

Amen.

On the Threshold

*So the man took his concubine and sent her outside to them, and
they raped her and abused her throughout the night, and at dawn
they let her go. At daybreak the woman went back to the house where
her master was staying, fell down at the door and lay there until
daylight.*

*When her master got up in the morning and opened the door of
the house and stepped out to continue on his way, there lay his
concubine, fallen in the doorway of the house, with her hands on the
threshold.*

JUDGES 19:25-27

Heavenly Father,

It's painful even to read about this kind of cruelty and violence. But because You include stories like this one in the Bible, we know that You
don't callously turn away from ugly realities. Instead, You shine the
truth on such dark corners as these, exposing what is evil to the light.
And You ask us to do the same (Eph. 5:11).

You alone, Lord, know how many wives—and husbands too—have
suffered from traumatic or hurtful experiences at the hands of others.
You fully comprehend how such events can leave a painful legacy of distrust, fear, and anger that can haunt a marriage for years. Today this is
our prayer: Please reveal to us how serious wounds from the past may
still be affecting our relationship.

Thank You for Your promise that we *can* put the past behind us
and go forward to better things (Isa. 43:18-19). We want to cooperate
with Your healing miracles. Show us where unforgiveness might be

keeping us bitter and bound (Heb. 12:15), where an ongoing conflict needs healthy closure (Eph. 4:31), or where we can take any brave, hard steps toward change (2 Tim. 1:7).

Come, Lord, with healing in Your wings (Mal. 4:2)! Bind up our wounds (Ps. 147:3)—be they from family, friends, or strangers. When we are lying on the threshold, bruised and brokenhearted, carry our sorrow and pain (Isa. 53:4). How much we need to hear Your tender voice saying, *I have chosen you and have not rejected you. So do not fear, for I am with you* (Isa. 41:9-10).

At times like these we are so grateful, Father, for the healing gift of our marriage. You inhabit our love for each other with Your redemptive power. You are always working in us (Phil. 2:13)! As we give and receive, as we injure and are forgiven, You are patiently helping us learn new lessons of love and trust.

In this process give us compassion for each other, especially when progress takes longer than we'd like. Give us the tender wisdom of Jesus to know what to say or do when the one we love is hurting (John 11:17-40) or to hear the real message behind our mate's emotional outpourings or silent withdrawals.

Right now, we release to You every wrong or evil others have committed against us. Free us to receive all the love You long to lavish upon us (1 John 3:1).

Thank You for Your promise that though tears endure for a night, joy comes in the morning (Ps. 30:5). May we soon be sharing that comfort and joy with others who need it (2 Cor 1:5-7).

Amen.

Whiners from Egypt

They forgot . . . the wonders he had shown them. . . . They spoke against God, saying, "Can God spread a table in the desert?" . . . Yet he was merciful; he forgave their iniquities and did not destroy them.

PSALM 78:11,19,38

PRAYING FROM PSALM 78

Lord,

How did You do it? How did You put up with Your people's relentless whining? And how do You put up with all of our complaining when we're so blessed by You?

We don't want to be like the Israelites whom You led out of Egypt. In spite of Your provision, they kept on grumbling. And in spite of Your wonders, they did not believe (v. 32). Again and again they doubted Your goodness and power—and demanded that You prove Yourself one more time (v. 41).

But You had mercy on them (v. 38). Thank You, patient Lord. That's why I can be honest with You in prayer right now. We, too, need Your mercy. Forgive us for the streak of self-absorbed, small-minded un-gratefulness that runs so deep in both of us. Forgive us when we act like whiners from Egypt dreaming of "the good old days":

—before the kids came and we lost so much free time;

—before this or that health problem slowed us down;

—before we had such a big mortgage;

—before . . .

Lord, we don't want to miss what good gifts You're ready to give us right now because we're wandering around the house whining about what we used to have. Show us that underneath our comfortable habits of complaining lurk serious sins like rebellion (v. 17), betrayal (v. 37), and unbelief (v. 22).

Merciful Lord, today we turn away from any kind of discontent that would keep us tied to yesterday and unable to receive Your promises for today. We do remember who You are! We remember Your miracles and Your redemption (v. 42). Today, Lord, our eyes are on You with faith and trust. "We will tell the next generation the praiseworthy deeds of the LORD, his power, and the wonders he has done" (v. 4).

Thank You, Lord, that the Promised Land is as close as our willingness to love, trust, and obey You wholeheartedly.

Amen.

Ambassadors

For Christ's love compels us, because we are convinced that one died for all, and therefore all died. And he died for all, that those who live should no longer live for themselves but for him who died for them and was raised again.

2 CORINTHIANS 5:14-15

PRAYING FROM 2 CORINTHIANS 5-6

Lord Jesus,

Today we pray that the love You lavish on us would compel us to love others (5:14). Make our marriage a ministry in the greatest sense: that we would together be ambassadors of Your saving love (v. 15)!

Remind us that the people we meet every day are souls You love and desire to reach (v. 16). Thank You that we are already Your new creations, Lord. You have decided not to count our sins against us, and You have rescued us from living an empty, pointless life (v. 18).

Now Christ's love compels us—and we have a marriage with a mission. We are Your ambassadors, as surely as those who travel to foreign countries to represent their king. How incredible to think that You are making Your appeal to this world through us (v. 20).

Show us how to effectively share Your message of reconciliation. Help us to boldly proclaim the good news: "God made him who had no sin to be sin for us, so that in him we might become the righteousness of God" (v. 21).

As Your ambassadors today, show us practical ways to speak up for

You—a friendly phone call, a kind invitation, a favor, a hug, a prayer. With all our hearts we want to make a powerful appeal for You because "now is the time of God's favor, now is the day of salvation" (6:2).

Amen.

Fish-Belly Prayers

You brought my life up from the pit, O LORD my God.

JONAH 2:6

Blessed Redeemer,

What can we say today except, "Help!"? We're in deep trouble! Like Jonah who chose to flee to Tarshish after You told him to go to Nineveh, we have chosen to go our own way. Now my spouse and I are inside the belly of a fish, swallowed whole by the trouble our sin has caused. Waves engulf us, the deep surrounds us. There's seaweed wrapped around our heads (Jon. 2:5).

Help us remember that it doesn't matter who's to blame. We're in this fish together, offering up this fish-belly prayer, a plea for Your mercy: You who sent the storm into Jonah's life (1:4), give us grace in our storm now; You who hurled him into the deep (2:3), have mercy on us; You who sent the fish to swallow him whole (1:17), we look to You for rescue (2:4).

God of second chances, just as You forgave Jonah of his rebellion, we come to You in confidence that You will not despise a broken spirit and a contrite heart (Ps. 51:17). Thank You, Lord, that if we confess our sins You are faithful and just and will forgive us—and purify us from all our stupid mistakes (1 John 1:9).

We ask You to restore to us the joy of our salvation and grant us willing spirits to sustain us (Ps. 51:12). And we wait in faith, believing in Your promise of grace and mercy to Your children whom You invite to come boldly before Your throne (Heb. 4:16).

Thank You, gracious Lord. In Your name we pray. Amen.

When Miracles Knock

Peter knocked at the outer entrance, and a servant girl named Rhoda came to answer the door. When she recognized Peter's voice, she was so overjoyed she ran back without opening it and exclaimed, "Peter is at the door!"

"You're out of your mind," they told her. When she kept insisting that it was so, they said, "It must be his angel."

AFTER AN ANGEL SET PETER FREE FROM PRISON, ACTS 12:13-15

Lord,

This is so like us! We pray and pray, and when You finally answer us, we can hardly believe it. The very thing we've been praying for has come to pass, and we are shocked that You have come through. Please forgive our small, foolish faith.

Has an answer to some urgent need already arrived today?

Is the miracle we long for already standing at the door?

You've warned us that if we see with faithless eyes, our whole lives will be filled with darkness (Matt. 6:23). Today we pray for the kind of faith that opens every door, fully expecting Your answer!

Today hear our prayers, especially for _____. And help us to confidently expect Your response. Thank You, Lord, that You are not too good to be true!

Amen.

A Blessing for Overcoming Temptation

I bless you in Jesus' name, my dear marriage partner, to overcome temptation today. May you experience firsthand God's trustworthiness and caring in your time of testing. May you see the way of escape and take it—and celebrate your deliverance with me soon!

FROM 1 CORINTHIANS 10:13

False Appeals

No temptation has seized you except what is common to man. And God is faithful; he will not let you be tempted beyond what you can bear. But when you are tempted, he will also provide a way out so that you can stand up under it.

Heavenly Father,

We are facing temptation. We're up against forces stronger than us—and some of them we can't even see! Our own desires entice us, the world beckons, and Satan roars like a lion (1 John 2:16, 1 Pet. 5:8). O Father, save us!

Don't let evil wound or trap us today. Make a way of escape, as You've promised (1 Cor. 10:13). By Your power, block any evil people who might be influencing our desires and actions (Ps. 140:1). Help us to see through the false appeal that could be endangering us, blinding us to the truth (James 1:15).

Turn our eyes away from worthless things; refresh our commitments to You (Ps. 119:37). Bring Your Word, hidden in our memories, to mind at critical moments. Use it to quickly challenge and redirect any decisions that could take us down the wrong path (Ps. 119:11).

Thank You that You are a faithful Savior who rescues Your own (2 Pet. 2:9). All attractions but You fade away (Ps. 102:12). Show us again today that as we make You our delight, You will give us the *real* desires of our hearts (Ps. 37:4).

Amen.

We're Not Worried

Until now you haven't asked for anything in my name. Ask and you will receive, and your joy will be complete.

JOHN 16:24

DAILY MEDITATIONS

Heavenly Father,
Thank You that have You invited us to present our requests to You in the power of Your own Son's name. Instead of worrying today—which never helps anyway—we choose to pray in Jesus' name (Matt. 6:27, Phil. 4:6). Dear Father, let these promises of Your provision resonate in our spirits all day long and bring us joy.

   Amen.

For practical needs:

"We will not worry, saying,
'What shall we eat?' or 'What shall we drink?'
Our heavenly Father knows what we need."
(from Matt. 6:31-32)

For spiritual power:

"God will meet all of our needs
according to his glorious riches
in Christ Jesus."
(from Phil. 4:19)

For peace and security:

"We will cast all of our anxiety on him,
because he cares for us!"
(from 1 Pet. 5:7)

1,001 Trifles

ry to imagine what our prayer experience would be like if he had forbidden us to ask for the little things. What if the only things we were allowed to talk about were the weighty matters, the important things, the profound issues? We would be orphaned in the cosmos, cold, and terribly alone. But the opposite is true: he welcomes us with our 1,001 trifles, for they are each important to him.

RICHARD FOSTER

Judas and Me

When Judas, who had betrayed him, saw that Jesus was condemned, he was seized with remorse and returned the thirty silver coins to the chief priests and the elders. "I have sinned," he said, "for I have betrayed innocent blood."

MATTHEW 27:3-4

Lord Jesus,

It's so hard for me to understand Judas's betrayal and suicide. Did he expect things to turn out differently? Was he trying to force You to take political power, not dreaming that You would let Yourself be crucified?

But in a hundred different ways I *am* Judas, completely capable of betraying Your friendship. I, too, rebel when You don't seem to take aggressive action on my behalf.

Please forgive me for my prideful assumptions about Your will or for self-centered questions about Your methods. Help my mate and me to remember that Your kingdom—and Your area of great concern for us   is not primarily this physical world but the eternal, spiritual realm (2 Cor. 4:18).

And when we do fail You, Lord, help us not to make Judas's greatest mistake—underestimating Your amazing lovingkindness and readiness to forgive. Thank You, Lord, that You would have forgiven Judas if he'd asked. Even after Peter betrayed You three times, You forgave and restored him (John 21:15-19). You are kind and forgiving, abounding in love to all who call to You (Ps. 86:5).

Keep us from betrayals of all kinds. May we never run from

You or each other in the futile agony of self-condemnation. But may our remorse lead us back to Your mercies, because "godly sorrow brings repentance that leads to salvation and leaves no regret" (2 Cor. 7:10).

Amen.

Champion of Love

The LORD is acting as the witness between you and the wife of your youth, because you have broken faith with her, though she is your partner, the wife of your marriage covenant. Has not the LORD made them one? In flesh and spirit they are his.

MALACHI 2:14-15

PRAYING FROM MALACHI 2

Lord,

We know that You hate divorce (Mal. 2:16). Not just because we break Your rules when we end a marriage but because we break Your heart as well as our own. How much we grieve You when we betray and reject the person we have committed ourselves to in love (v. 10).

Thank You for both the warning and the comfort we find in the words of Your prophet Malachi. How glad we are that You actively defend both of us and contend for our marriage. You stand by any wife who is rejected or any husband whose wife has broken faith with him somehow (v. 14).

Because we are Yours, Lord, in body and spirit, we choose today to hate what You hate. We commit today never to consider the course of divorce as a solution to our problems. If we have been made one by You, who are we to separate what You've created and what belongs to You (v. 15)?

Please be the defender and champion of our love even in the small things today. You are our hope. Teach us how to care for and treasure each other as much You do.

Amen.

Humble Pie

All of you, clothe yourselves with humility toward one another, because, "God opposes the proud but gives grace to the humble."

1 PETER 5:5

Lord,

I need Your help to change my clothing today. I confess that I wake up arrogant; my first thoughts toward my mate are arrogant—and so are my second thoughts . . .

I long to have the kind of humble spirit that Peter describes. But somehow, I'm usually inclined to haughtiness, to thinking more of myself than I ought (Rom. 12:3). How can someone who struggles with self-worth one moment be so sure of his superiority the next?

Loving Lord, I want to be like You, clothed with humility and grace. Even though You are God of the universe, You willingly took on human form and submitted Yourself to insults, disgrace, and death so we could have eternal life (Phil. 2:8).

Right now, I want to trade my rags of pride and arrogance for Your lovely garments. Grow in my spirit a deep respect for my mate's point of view (Phil. 2:4). And help me be quick to consider that I might be wrong. When I am wrong, help me to eat my "humble pie" with a smile, knowing that humility comes before honor (Prov. 18:12).

Amen.

How Love Grows

A happiness that is sought for ourselves alone can never be found: for a happiness that is diminished by being shared is not big enough to make us happy.

There is a false and momentary happiness in self-satisfaction, but it always leads to sorrow because it narrows and deadens our spirit. True happiness is found in unselfish love, a love which increases in proportion as it is shared.

THOMAS MERTON

A Wife Named Patience

*But I will establish my covenant with you, and you will enter the ark—
you and your sons and your wife and your sons' wives with you.*

A WIFE'S PRAYER

Lord,

Teach me today through Noah's wife, a woman whose name is never
mentioned in Scripture. Was her name Patience?

When Noah's wife realized that You, Lord, were saving her family
from a catastrophic flood (Heb. 11:7), she must have been terrified and
saddened and yet overwhelmed with gratitude.

But did she ever grow weary and lose sight of Your promise during
the years that followed? It took so long to gather the building materials,
longer to build the strange boat, and longer still to gather food and animals (Gen. 6:9-7:12). And all the while, how did Patience explain the
ridiculous goings-on to her friends and neighbors? Was she smiling or
crying?

During the dreary months aboard the ark, how did Patience endure
it—cooped up as she was with all those noisy, messy, smelly animals day
after day? Had her dream of married life come to—*this!?* Did she complain to Noah when she fell exhausted into their makeshift bunk at
night? Or despite her fatigue, was she still able to share his dreams, care
about his desires, listen to his doubts—and trust You?

I wonder, Lord, during those years and afterward did Patience simply go about her life each day in faith, hope, and love?

Lord, I remember rejoicing over our wedding promises—love, honor, obey. I remember thinking that our marriage and our family would be one of a kind, a little ark stuffed with miracles floating across the troubled waters of the world . . .

But it has taken more time and effort than I expected.

It has been less remarkable and romantic than I thought.

It has been more like a man and a woman in cramped, soggy, stuffy quarters, holding on to hope, to love, and to Your promises . . . and waiting for blue skies.

Lord, I just want to be a wife named Patience. Let faith make me strong today and every day, no matter how often or how long troubles seem to rain down on our family. I want to be a "hero of faith" in this joint venture of marriage. Help me to endure confidently so that Your promises will have time to be fulfilled and You can bless generations to come through me.

Do not throw away your confidence; it will be richly rewarded. You need to persevere so that when you have done the will of God, you will receive what he has promised (Heb. 10:35-36).

Thank You, Lord.

Amen.

Knight Moves

The noble man makes noble plans, and by noble deeds he stands.

ISAIAH 32:8

A HUSBAND'S PRAYER

Heavenly Father,
Today I ask You to help me become the hero, a "knight in shining armor," who lives at this address. Not for acclaim, Lord, but to be Your champion. I want to be one who makes praiseworthy plans and follows through with them even when it hurts. By Your grace and enablement, I want to answer the call to do the good, hard deeds that building a God-honoring home requires.

Lord, I'm willing to start at the bottom of this "becoming a noble man" business. Your Word teaches that small steps toward a good end matter and that humility always precedes honor (Prov. 18:12, Matt. 23:12). Show me the small steps You have in mind for me today. And please, Lord, help me to do them silently and invisibly, if possible—not to clank around and rattle my sword to get admiration.

May I be the one who "will never be shaken" (Ps. 15:5) because You are at work making a shining knight from the rust and dust of my life. By Your precious renewing Spirit, make me like Jesus, who "humbled himself and became obedient to death—even death on a cross!" (Phil. 2:8). And help me to learn from the gallery of heroes who have gone before me:

—Job, who maintained his integrity even in the face of bankruptcy and death (Job 2:3);

—Samuel, who refused to take advantage of his position to defraud his people (1 Sam. 12:3);

—David, who was unafraid of giants because he trusted in Your power (1 Sam. 17:37);

—Daniel, whose enemies could find nothing to say against him because "he was trustworthy and neither corrupt nor negligent" (Dan. 6:4);

—Timothy, who guarded what had been entrusted to him and held on to faith and a good conscience (1 Tim. 1:19, 6:20);

—Philemon, one who had a reputation for loving and caring for other believers (Philem. 5,7).

Father, these "knight moves" take a lifetime to learn. Apart from Your power in me, they are impossible (John 15:5). But I surrender to Your miracle today. And I throw the weight of my commitment to the task.

My wife and my family deserve nothing less than a noble man walking around in my shoes today, one who is busy all day making noble plans, doing noble deeds . . . and trying not to clank.

Amen.

True Calling

With this in mind, we constantly pray for you, that our God may count you worthy of his calling, and that by his power he may fulfill every good purpose of yours and every act prompted by your faith.

2 THESSALONIANS 1:11

Lord,

Sometimes we wonder if our lives together are really adding up to something—or have we compromised Your calling for money, security, or ease? We want with all our hearts to be worthy servants for Your purposes.

Today we pray we will hear Your call and follow it without compromise—not just to *do* for You but to *become* like You. Remind us that we are:

—*called to be free* (Gal. 5:13). May we never get bound up in legalistic thinking but keep returning to the truth of Your grace so that we will serve You based on freedom, not on false guilt.

—*called out of darkness* (1 Pet. 2:9). May we keep a clean conscience every day so that we can be guided always by Your light.

—*called according to Your purpose* (Rom. 8:28). May we remember—even on those bad days when it looks like everything is going wrong—that You are willing and able to work all these messy circumstances together for our good and for Your perfect purposes.

Thank You for calling us, Lord!
Amen.

Glory's Glow

I have given them the glory that you gave me, that they may be one as we are one.

MEDITATIONS TO CARRY THROUGH THE DAY

Lord,
Help us look intently across the table into each other's eyes—and see a radiance we might have missed yesterday.
    Amen.

We whose faces reflect the Lord's glory
are being transformed
into his likeness with an ever-increasing glory
that comes from the Lord Himself!
(from 2 Cor. 3:18)

We are confident that our present sufferings—
financial, relational, or physical—
are nothing
compared to the future glory that God has promised.
(from Rom. 8:18)

"That's Not Fair!"

But if you suffer for doing good and you endure it, this is commendable before God.

1 PETER 2:20

Lord Jesus,

No one knows better than You what it's like to be misunderstood or unfairly treated. You warned us that everyone who wants to live in harmony with You *will* experience mistreatment from those who oppose You (2 Tim. 3:12). Yet it's the unfairnesses we experience at the hands of our own flesh and blood that hurt most.

Show me today what it means to rejoice in every trial for Your sake (James 1:2-3). When my spouse reacts unfairly in some way, help me to remember that You are always for me—*and* my marriage (Ps. 9:10).

Most of all, help me not to make things worse by returning injury for injury but to pay back with a blessing (1 Pet. 3:9). You've promised that when we suffer for doing right, You will reward us (1 Pet. 2:20).

And Lord, please open my eyes to this troubling possibility—that these supposed wrongs actually begin with me, with how I'm behaving or how I'm perceiving things. At these times, be kindly stubborn with me! I really do want to see things in a true light. And, with Your help, I'm ready to change.

In the meantime, cover us all with Your patient and forgiving love—so costly yet so free with each new day (Ps. 23:6).

Amen.

A Psalm for Our House

Praise the LORD. Praise the LORD, O my soul. I will praise the LORD
all my life; I will sing praise to my God as long as I live.

PSALM 146:1-2

PRAYING PSALM 146

Lord,

We sing praises to You from this house today. Because of You, we can
experience a marriage of enduring hope and confident trust. No boss,
government, job, money supply, or other power is our source of security—they can disappear overnight (vv. 3-4). No, it is You, "Maker of
heaven and earth, the sea, and everything in them" who are our confidence! You remain faithful forever (v. 6)! We worship and celebrate
You today.

Listen to our family's testimony of praise about You, O Lord,
our God:

You uphold the cause of the oppressed (v. 7). When we've been surrounded on every side, You have been our champion; You have rescued
us from trouble after trouble (Ps. 118:11-13).

You give food to the hungry (v. 7). When we've needed food for body
or soul, You have been our provider. You have been a renewing source
of life to us (Ps. 23:2-3, 103:5).

You set prisoners free (v. 7). When we were captives to sin and despair, You brought us life (John 8:36, Rom. 8:1-2).

You give sight to the blind (v. 8). When we couldn't see to know the way home or to know what to do, You opened our eyes and gave us guidance (Isa. 42:6-7).

You lift up those who are bowed down (v. 8). When we have been discouraged and overburdened by life, even by our marriage, You have kindly lifted us up and carried us like a Father (Deut. 1:30-31, Ps. 28:8-9).

You love the righteous (v. 8). When we have doubted that being Your children was worth the suffering it's brought, You have broken through our fears to reveal Your personal passion for each of us (Psalm 73, 116:1-7, 1 Pet. 1:3-9).

You watch over the alien and sustain the fatherless and the widow (v. 9). When we or those we know and love have faced loss and loneliness of all kinds, we have found You to be a refuge and protector (Ps. 23:4, John 14:18, Deut. 31:6).

But You frustrate the ways of the wicked (v. 9). The older we get, the more we see that those easy, wrong paths that looked so good end up in trouble and grief. But the path of obedience to You shines brighter and brighter every day (Prov. 4:18-19).

You, Lord, will reign forever, and with our praises today we again crown You Lord of our marriage and our family—and pray that You will reign supreme in our house for generations to come (v. 10).

Amen.

Listening Lessons

He who answers before listening—that is his folly and his shame.

Lord,

I am certainly a fool. How many times a day I answer before I listen! Instead of being quick to hear, I race to speak (James 1:19).

Lord, Your ears are never too dull to hear (Isa. 59:1). But mine are often so dull that I miss most of what is being said. And if I can't hear the audible and sometimes loud voice of my partner, how will I hear the still, small voice of my Lord?

How can I change, Lord? Today this is my prayer: Give me ears to hear (Matt. 11:15). Give me a heart that waits (1 Cor. 13:4). Give me a tongue that hesitates (Prov. 10:19).

Please help me to listen even to words I don't really want to hear. Behind my partner's complaints, let me hear his or her disappointments. Behind long stories that seem to derail, let me hear the memories and dreams that mean the most to him or her. Behind seemingly unfair reproaches, let me hear a valid hurt.

And behind our companionable silences, help me hear love.

Amen.

Stone of Help

Then Samuel took a stone and set it up between Mizpah and Shen. He named it Ebenezer ["stone of help"], saying, "Thus far has the LORD helped us."

1 SAMUEL 7:12

Heavenly Father, Rock of Ages,
You are powerful! You are immovable! You are strong! No wonder Your people have called You their Rock. Today we raise our "Ebenezer" of praise to You, our Rock.

With Samuel we say, "Thus far has the LORD helped us!" Thank You, Father, that You are a "stone of help"—a trustworthy source of rescue and provision in times of trouble.

With Moses we declare, "Oh, praise the greatness of our God! He is the Rock, his works are perfect, and all his ways are just" (Deut. 32:3-4). Thank You, Lord, that because everything You do is exactly right and fair, we can wait patiently for You to reveal Your purposes to us.

With Isaiah we sing, "We will trust in the LORD forever, for the LORD, the LORD, is the Rock eternal" (from Isa. 26:4). Because You're our eternal Rock, we will always rely on You to be the foundation of our marriage and to be a fortress for our souls forever!

Today with David we pray, "May the words of our mouths, and the meditations of our hearts be pleasing in your sight, O LORD, our Rock, our Redeemer" (from Ps. 19:14).

Amen.

Fathers Like to Be Asked

here is] the very reasonable question of why we should ask God for things when he already knows our needs. The most straightforward answer to this question is simply that God likes to be asked. We like our children to ask us for things that we already know they need because the very asking enhances and deepens the relationship. P. T. Forsyth notes, "Love loves to be told what it knows already. . . . It wants to be asked for what it longs to give."

RICHARD FOSTER

The Good Wife

She brings him good, not harm, all the days of her life.

PROVERBS 31:12

A WIFE'S PRAYER

Father,

Did I read that right? A wife is to bring her husband good all the days of her life? Seems like a tall order, one I don't seem very good at filling.

Those who plan what is good find love and faithfulness (Prov. 14:22).

Father, help me come up with a plan. All the women's magazines burst with advice on catching, dating, even marrying a man, but they don't tell me how to bring him good. Where do I start? Are there ten easy steps? Should I bake a cake? Meet him in a new dress?

Your beauty should not come from outward adornment. . . . Instead, it should be that of your inner self, the unfading beauty of a gentle and quiet spirit (1 Pet. 3:3-4).

I long for that kind of inner goodness, Lord, but most of the time my personality gets in the way. My bad moods and self-centeredness only tear him down. How can I try harder? I care so much about this.

Not by might nor by power, but by my Spirit, says the LORD Almighty (Zech. 4:6). *The fruit of the Spirit is . . . goodness* (Gal. 5:22).

You're right, Lord. Your goodness working through me today can bring good to my husband. By Your Spirit show me creative ways to express Your goodness to him all the days of my life.

A cake would be a good place to start, don't You think?

In Your name I pray. Amen.

Ordinary Guy

The LORD is my strength and my song.

EXODUS 15:2

A HUSBAND'S PRAYER

Loving Lord,

Today is a masterpiece that You have made, and You already know everything that will happen today (Ps. 118:24, 139:16). You are the great Creator God—nothing is impossible for You (Luke 1:37).

But I'm the original "Ordinary Guy." I don't think I can be the husband my wife deserves today. My motivation and even my good intentions feel at a low ebb. I acknowledge two truths today—Your power and my weakness. Forgive me, my God, and hear my prayer.

When my arms get too tired today to comfort my wife, please give me Your strength. Thank You that Your strong, caring arms are always underneath us to carry us (Deut. 33:27). Be like a father to her, carrying her in Your arms as You did the children of Israel (Deut. 1:30-31).

Sometimes it's hard on my pride, but even my wife knows the truth: I can do nothing without You, Lord (John 15:5). How glad I am that You promise to renew my strength if I hope in You (Isa. 40:31).

As Paul did, I choose to rejoice in my weaknesses today, knowing You will step up and reveal Your own power (2 Cor. 12:9). And when others see me—an ordinary husband—serving my wife by Your strength, may they give You the praise You deserve (1 Pet. 4:11).

Amen.

In-Laws and Outlaws

Moses listened to his father-in-law and did everything he said.

EXODUS 18:24

Heavenly Father,

Thank You that when You chose my mate, You also chose my in-laws. You knew exactly who they were and whether it would be an easy match or a tough one.

Lord, both of us want to live out our faith by being a blessing to our extended families, especially our in-laws. Your Word says that if we neglect to care for our relatives, we are betraying our commitment to You (1 Tim. 5:8).

Teach us the loyalty of Ruth, who left her own home to follow her widowed mother-in-law to a new land (Ruth 1:16-17). May we, too, care deeply and sacrificially for the parents who gave life to the one we love so dearly. May we honor and provide for them as long as they live, as if they were our own parents.

Teach us the respectful tolerance of David, whose father-in-law, Saul, behaved more like an outlaw than "the Lord's anointed." Repeatedly Saul tried to kill David, yet repeatedly David spared the king's life and continued to show him respect (1 Samuel 24). May we, too, show forbearance toward our in-laws—even when we feel that they don't deserve it. May we be careful how we speak to and about them and continually pursue peace and unity.

Finally, Lord, teach us the humility of Moses, who listened carefully to his father-in-law's advice in the middle of a difficult situation (Exod. 18:24). May we, too, be willing to hear the observations and suggestions of our in-laws. Keep us from the kind of pride that says, "I don't need your advice!"

In all these ways, Lord, may we honor our spouses and Your purposes for marriage by honoring our extended families. Use our experiences with them to strengthen our understanding of each other, to bind us closer together in love, and to bring glory to You.

Amen.

Tread Softly Here

have spread my dreams under

your feet;

Tread softly because you tread

on my dreams.

WILLIAM BUTLER YEATS

The Cover–Up

Even though we were dead in our sins God, who is rich in mercy,
because of the great love he had for us, gave us life together with Christ.

EPHESIANS 2:4-5, PH

O Lord God, rich in mercy . . .
Yes, of all the beauties that surround You, Lord, Your mercies are the
most lovely to me today. I need them most. Your love and Your forgiveness weave a covering of hope for me and my family (1 Pet. 1:3). Yes,
You are gracious, good, and full of compassion (Ps. 116:5).

Today in my marriage I pray for the gift of mercy—in my
thoughts, in my reflexes, in my expectations, in my words, in my sense
of humor. I pray for a treasure chest overflowing with it!

Unlike You, Lord, I can only extend mercy because I need it so
much myself. When I had earned the death penalty, You set me free
and expunged my record. And every day, when I continue to run up
debts, You continue to set my bill at zero—"Paid in full" (Eph. 2:4-9).

Lord, so beautiful in Your lovingkindnesses, help me never to be
like the unmerciful servant who, forgiven much himself, turned around
to require much of another (Matt. 18:21-35).

Love forgets mistakes. . . . Love overlooks insults. . . . Love does not
hold grudges (Prov. 17:9, 10:12, 1 Cor. 13:5, TLB).

Lord, shine Your light on any unforgiving attitudes in my heart today, and fill my heart with mercy for my beloved spouse (Heb. 4:16).

In Jesus' name I pray, Amen.

Drawing Near

Let us draw near to God with a sincere heart in full assurance of faith.

HEBREWS 10:22

O Lord God,

We draw near to You today. We wait confidently in this "Most Holy Place" because Jesus has opened "a new and living way" for us to come to You (Heb. 10:19-20). He is our great high priest. Thank You that even when we feel dingy, Christ wraps us in perfect white. Because of Him, as ordinary as we are, we know that Your arms, Father, are open wide to welcome us (vv. 21-22).

You are near, as You've promised (James 4:8). You are as real as gold in Fort Knox, and You reward us with even greater treasure when we earnestly seek You (Heb. 11:6).

Today, Lord, we plead for Your mercy and grace on our marriage in our time of need (Heb. 4:16). Yes, God of the universe, we come boldly because our poverty is so pressing and because Your "blessing is our greatest wealth" (Prov. 10:22, TLB).

Thank You for hearing our prayer, as You always do (John 11:42). Thank You that through Jesus Christ we have eternal access to You even though Your holiness and power are completely beyond our understanding and our worthiness to receive (Eph. 2:18).

Draw near to us now as we humbly draw near to You.

In Jesus' dear name. Amen.

The Gratitude Attitude

It is good to give thanks to the LORD, and to sing praises to Thy name,
O Most High; to declare Thy lovingkindness in the morning, and Thy
faithfulness by night.

PSALM 92:1-2, NASB

O heavenly Lord,

You have been good to me. You have surrounded me with Your favor
like a shield (Ps. 5:12). Because of Your blessings, our family's needs are
met and many of our deepest desires are satisfied (Deut. 12:7).

Today I thank You for my marriage partner—the completer of my
self and a continuing expression of Your goodness in my life. Thank
You for making us one (Gen. 2:24), and thank You for leading us
toward a deeper union despite all of our shortcomings.

You have given me a friend who favors me with patience, honesty,
tenderness, and good humor. Every morning I am blessed by my mate's
steadying influence, hard work, and faithful shouldering of responsibil-
ity. Every evening I am comforted by our shared companionship, kindness, and affection.

Praise for You will be on the tip of my tongue all day (Ps. 34:1) because You are a generous God, and Your love for my family never stops
(Ps. 136:1). I will worship You today with a contented heart (1 Tim.
6:6) because this is the marriage You have given me and the one You are
ready to bless if I seek You (Ps. 119:2).

And I do!

May my attitude of gratitude be a source of strength to me all day
and a source of pleasure for You (Ps. 51:12).

Amen.

The Sound of Burning Bridges

Forgetting what is behind and straining toward what is ahead, I press on toward the goal to win the prize for which God has called me heavenward in Christ Jesus.

PHILIPPIANS 3:13-14

Lord Jesus,

In my marriage today I want to press ahead. And to go forward, first I need Your help to "leave" what is behind (Gen. 2:24). Leaving my parents behind wasn't too hard. But for the marriage partner You've given me, I want to burn any bridges to my past that would hinder us from moving ahead:

—old expectations

—inappropriate loyalties

—immature pastimes

—harmful grudges and foolish regrets

Every day I want to walk resolutely into the future You have in mind for us. This marriage—with all its oddities, absurdities, and wonders—is part of Your divine plan. It is an integral part of how Your redemption will come to us, to many we meet along the way, and to generations to come (Ps. 71:18).

Lord Jesus, burn my bridges! Let me hear the roar and smell the smoke today. I'm not going back. Thank You for Your promise I carry with me: The Lord delights in the way of a man (or woman) whose steps he has made firm; though he (or she) stumble, he will not fall, for the Lord upholds him (or her) with his hand (from Ps. 37:23-24).

By Your power and grace. Amen.

Unfailing Love

Though the mountains be shaken and the hills be removed, yet my unfailing love for you will not be shaken.

ISAIAH 54:10

Lord,

You know how much we long to experience an unfailing love (Prov. 19:22). Your Word promises us that true love never fails (1 Cor. 13:8). But so often our own love for each other falls short. In fact, it falls flat on its face. Many a person claims to have unfailing love, but a faithful man or woman who can find? (from Prov. 20:6).

Help us, dear Lord! We know that love doesn't fail us, but *we* fail to love. Our own human attempts get waylaid by our selfishness and ulterior motives.

Today this is our prayer: Dwell in our pitiful attempts to love one another without fail. By Your Spirit break up the hard ground of our hearts. Water the little seeds of love we do manage to sow—small kindnesses, tender words, patience with each other's faults.

Thank You, Lord, that Your love never, ever fails, even when we do. All day long, "May your unfailing love rest upon us, O LORD, even as we put our hope in you" (Ps. 33:22).

Amen.

Eyes of Grace

To love is not to view someone as being the most wonderful person in the world or to think of them as a saint. On the contrary, it may mean to see them as we must come to see ourselves, even as the "chief of sinners." It is to see all their weakness, their falseness and shoddiness, to have all their very worst habits exposed—and then to be enabled, by the pure grace of God, not only to accept them, but to accept them in a deeper way than was ever before possible.

MIKE MASON

Married Peace

The wisdom that comes from heaven is first of all pure; then peace-loving, considerate, submissive, full of mercy and good fruit, impartial and sincere. Peacemakers who sow in peace raise a harvest of righteousness.

JAMES 3:17-18

Lord of Peace,

You say it is good and pleasant when we live together in harmony (Ps. 133:1), that a marriage divided against itself can't last (Matt. 12:25). But today I'm aware of things about my love relationship that aren't harmonious at all: teasing, silly quarrels, running arguments.

Lord, I want to choose the beautiful way of peace. Our marriage—however flawed it might seem at the moment—is worth more than anybody's right to win. I want to begin with the steppingstones to peace that James suggests. Help me to become:

First of all, pure — Cleanse me of pride and self-centeredness. Lord, this is so hard—even my desire for peace is mostly selfish. By the power of Your Spirit, purify my motives and thoughts.

Then peace-loving — Today, I'm willing to give up other good things—fairness, my "rights," my reasonable expectations—and reach for Your best. Help me to cherish what You cherish.

Considerate — Remind me of a need that my spouse might be feeling that I've forgotten recently. May I be sensitive to those feelings.

Submissive — How many of our differences are really power struggles! But You, Lord, came to serve. Your followers argued about who should be first, but You washed their feet. Help me to humbly put my mate first (Phil. 2:3).

Full of mercy and good fruit—Lord, I'm so quick with an opinion and so slow with a kind act. Please forgive me. Help me to show mercy cheerfully and to do kind deeds generously (Rom. 12:8).

Impartial and sincere— Sometimes I know I'm not judging my partner fairly, Lord. I favor my own brilliant opinions! Lord, help me to sincerely consider my mate's side of an issue when we differ.

Thank You for the promise of Your Word that those who are willing to pay the price for a life of peace will reap a harvest of good (James 3:18).

You are the God of peace; equip us with every good grace we need to be like You. May we be like the first Christians who lived together with one heart and mind (Acts 4:32). Then we will experience the joy You promise to those who love peace (Prov. 12:20).

Amen.

A Blessing for Unity in Marriage

May the God who gives endurance and encouragement give us a spirit of unity among ourselves as we follow Christ Jesus, so that with one heart and mouth we may glorify Him today.

FROM ROMANS 15:5-6

Stock in God

In his great mercy he has given us new birth into a living hope through the resurrection of Jesus Christ from the dead.

1 PETER 1:3

PRAYING FROM 1 PETER 1

God and Father of our Lord Jesus Christ,
Because of the resurrection of Your Son from the dead, You have given us the incredible inheritance of eternal life—our "living hope" (v. 3). How we thank You that this fortune doesn't consist of blue-chip stocks, treasury bonds, or being named in the will of a rich relative.

Our inheritance is so much greater! It can never fade, depreciate, or evaporate altogether with a bad turn in the economy. Thank You, Lord, that all we really treasure is kept safe in heaven by You (v. 4).

Today in our marriage we greatly rejoice in our wonderful inheritance—in spite of all the daily trials and pressures we're experiencing (v. 6). These troubles won't last. Yet by Your redeeming power, they are never "worthless" either—they only *add* to our treasure if we'll let them. You stand ready to use these trials to refine our faith, which is far more valuable than gold (v. 7).

We can't check any index to see how our stock in God is performing. We can't even see You, Lord. But we believe that our inheritance is more real than anything we can see with our eyes (v. 8). And how we love You for it! How glad we are to know that someday we'll fully take possession of the greatest prize of all, which is the salvation of our souls (v. 9).

In Your precious name we pray. Amen.

Blessed Bragging

How is your beloved better than others, most beautiful of women?

SONG OF SONGS 5:9

A WIFE'S PRAYER

Lord,

You know that when I first fell in love I was so sure that my husband was the most wonderful man ever made. I swooned and gushed about him endlessly to my girlfriends. "He is so handsome! And he is so smart and interesting!" (from Song of Songs 1:16). But I confess, Lord, that these days I'm as likely to complain about my husband as to brag.

Forgive me, Lord! How much my husband needs to know that I still prefer him to any other man. Some days I see in his eyes just how much he wants to hear me speak to him—and about him—with pride, respect, and affection in my voice.

Today I pray that You would bless me with the urge to brag—not with empty flattery but with specific, sincere praises (Rom. 12:9). Remind me of his unique strengths and all the ways he brightens my days. Let these qualities crowd out any critical thoughts that dog my mind.

Your Word teaches that what I choose to say has power for life or death (Prov. 18:21). I want to be *life* for my husband!

Show me opportunities to declare to anyone who will listen, "My husband is amazing compared to so many other men! I am so blessed" (from Song of Songs 5:10). And today, may my sweetheart overhear me telling a friend that I am indeed "faint with love" (Song of Songs 5:8).

Amen.

A Lily Among Thorns

Like a lily among thorns is my darling among the maidens.

SONG OF SONGS 2:2

A HUSBAND'S PRAYER

Father,
Thank You for the gift of a loving wife. Like a lily in a garden, she graces my life with mysterious expressions of Your beauty.

All day, help me to protect Your dearest earthly gift to me. Give me eyes to see the thorns that threaten her—worries, dangers, disappointments, harmful relationships, unresolved conversations, unfinished business of any sort.

Also, Lord, show me what actions, gestures, or words on my part can make her bleed. Give my rough hands the tenderness of new love and a fresh willingness to feel the thorns as she would.

May my wife glow all day with pure light—like a creamy Easter lily unfurling with praise—because Your beauty remains upon her and because I have cherished her as she deserves.

Help me, Lover of heaven, to find new ways to prove her true worth and new excuses to whisper the lily's secret in her ear: "Many women do noble things, but you surpass them all" (Prov. 31:29).

Amen.

The Waiting Place

Be still before the LORD and wait patiently for him; do not fret.

Dear Lord of my day,

In these moments of prayer I quiet my mind and set aside all the loose ends of our worries. You see every need here—the ones we don't even know about and the ones that grip our attention and put a stranglehold on our faith.

Right now I place before You especially _____.

Please take each concern—and take my watch and my calendar too. Unless I release them to You, Lord, You will never be sovereign here.

I want to be still before You. *Help* me to be still . . . and in this still-ness to wait on You, Sovereign God . . .

—until my spirit is really off my list and on my Lord;

—until I really encounter You afresh and hear You for today;

—until You have the freedom to accomplish what You want, when You want, in my life, in my marriage, and in our home.

It is good to wait quietly for You (Lam. 3:26). You never ignore or abandon Your children (John 14:18). Instead, You make Your presence known to us (Ps. 25:14), and You renew our strength so we can soar on eagles' wings (Isa. 40:31).

Help me to let go . . . and soar in Your presence all day.

Amen.

I, Me, Mine

[Love] . . . is not self-seeking.

1 CORINTHIANS 13:5

Lord Jesus,

I confess that today I come to You filled with me. Every pore in my body screams, "My needs! My wants! My way!" Why? Because I'm always the one who gives around here. When is it my turn?

Do not think of yourself more highly than you ought (Rom. 12:3). *Nobody should seek his own good, but the good of others* (1 Cor. 10:24).

Ouch! Your words sear my heart, Lord. I know I'm not the only one who tries. But what about the urgent needs I have that go unmet day after day? What do I do about them?

The LORD will guide You always; he will satisfy your needs in a sun-scorched land (Isa. 58:11).

Thank You for this promise, Lord. Today I do feel sun scorched. My heart feels like a dry and weary land where there is no water (Ps. 63:1). I'm thirsty, Lord. Hear my cry!

Yes, Lord, I acknowledge right now that only You can satisfy my needs in my marriage and in my life. Only You have living water (John 4:10). Only You can change the self-seeking me to an other-seeking me. That's the me I want to be.

I ask these things in Your name. Amen.

A Hospitable Heart

Today I imagined my inner self as a place crowded with pins and needles. How could I receive anyone in my prayer when there is no real place for them to be free and relaxed? When I am still so full of preoccupations, jealousies, angry feelings, anyone who enters will get hurt. . . . To pray for others means to offer others a hospitable place where I can really listen to their needs and pains. . . .

If I could have a gentle "interiority"—a heart of flesh and not of stone, a room with some spots on which one might walk barefooted—then God and my fellow humans could meet each other there. Then the center of my heart can become the place where God can hear the prayer for my neighbors and embrace them with his love.

HENRI J. NOUWEN

God Is Good

I will cause all my goodness to pass in front of you, and I will proclaim my name, the LORD, in your presence.

EXODUS 33:19

Lord,

You have been good to us. Our lives are trophies of Your kindnesses on display. When I look at my spouse, my family, my home, and the things You are accomplishing in and through us, I declare to all, "You are good, and what you do is good" (Ps. 119:68).

May I not miss one single evidence of Your goodness that passes in front of my eyes today. Because I trust in Your generosity and continual provisions, I will look for gifts from You—in many disguises—all day long, from morning to evening (Ps. 32:10, James 1:17, Lam. 3:22-23).

If trouble surrounds me on every side today, if I unexpectedly must face death or loss, even if the mountains suddenly vanish today—even then, Your goodness will remain and prevail! (Ps. 23:4, Isa. 54:10, Nah. 1:7).

By Your grace today, "I will tell of the kindness of the Lord, the deeds for which he is to be praised, according to all the Lord has done for us—yes, the many good things he has done for this house, according to his compassion and many kindnesses" (from Isa. 63:7).

Amen.

A Pleasing Obsession

Am I now trying to win the approval of men, or of God? Or am I trying to please men? If I were still trying to please men, I would not be a servant of Christ.

GALATIANS 1:10

Holy Lord,

I find myself pleasing others instinctively. I confess, I want to be liked, hopefully even admired. But my prayer today is that I would have a deep need, a growing desire, an obvious preoccupation, even an embarrassing obsession with pleasing You!

I think of You, Lord: You did and said nothing on Your own but just what Your Father taught You to do. "I always do what pleases Him," You declared to those startled Pharisees (John 8:28-29). I think of You, but I can't live up to Your example. If I could always be Spirit-controlled, I could always please You—but I can't (Rom. 8:8). Yet by Your mysterious resurrection power, I ask You to accomplish Your pleasure in my life and marriage (Rom. 8:11).

What would please You, Lord?

Submit to one another out of reverence for Me. Serve one another in love (from Eph. 5:21, Gal. 5:13).

Yes, Lord, that's what I desire! Help me to remember today that it pleases You when I please the precious partner You've given me. Show me in my relationship how to be a true servant—yes, one who meets the needs of another. Teach me to be more like You in my marriage: faithful in prayer (John 17), relentlessly compassionate (Luke 15:20), humbly meeting whatever human need You would if You were here (John 13:15).

You've promised that when I live to please You in my relationships, even serious conflicts will disappear (Prov. 16:7). Make me a pleaser today, for Your own pleasure, dear Master.

Amen.

Married Friends

A friend loves at all times.

PROVERBS 17:17

Lord and Friend,

Today I pray that You would show me how to be not just a marriage partner but also a friend. It's easy to forget that what first brought us together—in addition to physical attraction—was friendship. We liked each other, and we liked to do things together.

I never want that friendship to die, Lord. Remind me what it takes to be a true friend. Your Word says that a friend loves at all times—when it's easy and fun and when it's hard, painful, or tiring. Help me to love my mate when he or she wants to do something I don't or when it seems like we've already had every possible interesting conversation we can think of (years ago, I might add).

Renew our friendship, Lord. Genuine friendship mattered so much to You when You were on earth. Remind us each day, Lord, that friendship—sharing time, secrets, intimacy, interests (yes, and even sore throats and bad mornings)—is not optional in marriage but foundational.

Today show me one new way that You might be asking me to lay down my life for the one I love—a preference, a right, a convenience—because "greater love has no one than this, that he lay down his life for his friends" (John 15:13).

Amen.

The Gift of Understanding

I t is impossible to overemphasize the immense need humans have to be really listened to, to be taken seriously, to be understood. No one can develop freely in this world and find a full life without feeling understood by at least one person.

PAUL TOURNIER

Dripping Faucets

Finally . . . live in harmony with one another; be sympathetic, love as brothers, be compassionate and humble.

1 PETER 3:8

A WIFE'S PRAYER

Lord,

You know how I hate to complain about him, but . . . the lawn needs mowing, the back door still squeaks, the car makes a funny noise, and the kids want the basketball hoop raised.

You know how I hate to complain, but . . . I keep asking my husband to help me, nudging him, reminding him. But I can't get him to listen, no matter how loud I shout. Oh—and the kitchen faucet leaks. Drip, drip, drip.

Lord, I can't think of anything more irritating than—

A nagging wife is like water going drip, drip, drip (from Prov. 19:13, CEV).

Oh. I don't mean to nag, but I guess I do. It's just that I want things done. Now. And my husband doesn't seem to understand—or care.

When words are many, sin is not absent, but he who holds his tongue is wise. . . . Pleasant words are a honeycomb, sweet to the soul and healing to the bones (Prov. 10:19, 16:24).

Forgive me, Lord, for my constant stream of negative messages. Help me instead to be constructive, patient, believing the best, and good humored (Eph. 4:2). Turn my "dripping" habit into a stream of affirmation to the well-intentioned husband You've given me.

Even if the grass never gets mowed.

Amen.

Cave Days

*In the day of trouble he will keep me safe in his dwelling; he will hide
me in the shelter of his tabernacle.*

PSALM 27:5

A HUSBAND'S PRAYER

Dear heavenly Father,
I confess that I'm in retreat mode today. I've run out of emotional elastic. I just want to hide in the back of a cave and not come out. My wife, the sunshine of my life, is lost in storm clouds.

How I want to listen and to care, to be a lover and a peacemaker—but some days I'm not the problem *or* the answer. All my words only seem to create more thunder and lightning.

Jesus, even You withdrew some days—to a garden, the other side of the lake, or a lonely hillside (Matt. 26:36, Mark 3:7, Luke 5:16). You needed to be alone, to find emotional and spiritual refreshment from the Father before You could be useful to others.

Today turn my need to withdraw into an opportunity to experience Your renewal. Help me find a "cave" of my own—working with my hands, fishing, cleaning the garage—where I can hear from You and be replenished. Show me how to take this time for myself in such a way that I don't leave my wife feeling abandoned or rejected. Calm her storms today, Lord. Give her Your own all-surpassing peace (Phil. 4:7).

In the meantime, help me to wait patiently and confidently for the sunshine of my life to come out again—as I know she will.

In Your name I pray. Amen.

Thanks for Two

Give thanks in all circumstances, for this is God's will for you in Christ Jesus.

1 THESSALONIANS 5:18

Gracious Lord,

Thank You for my spouse. Thank You that I'm not alone, that I have a companion by my side, a burden bearer, and a friend (Gen. 2:24).

Thank You for the whispered "I love you's" at the end of the day and for secrets shared. Thank You for inside jokes, pet names, and dreams for two.

Thank You for someone to laugh with. Thank You for someone who cares. Thank You for someone who understands—or at least tries to. Thank You for someone to serve with so much pleasure.

Of course, it's not always easy or fun. Sometimes it's downright frustrating. But today I choose to thank You even for the hard things about my marriage: for life's trials that cause us to grow; for tight budgets that force us to depend on You; for petty annoyances that chip away at our rough edges; for hard times that cause us to cling as one to You.

How I thank You, Lord, for bringing us together! Together may we seek Your strength—because power belongs to You (Ps. 62:11, KJV).

Together may we bring honor to Your name—because there is no other name under heaven that brings us life (Acts 4:12).

Together may we offer You thanks—because Your goodness to us is beyond description (2 Cor. 9:15).

Thank You, Lord!

Amen.

Sleep Easy

I will lie down and sleep in peace, for you alone, O LORD, make me dwell in safety.

PSALM 4:8

PRAYING PSALM 91

Heavenly Father,
You know that sometimes I wake up in the night full of fears for my spouse. I imagine how quickly a car wreck or a diagnosis of cancer could snatch my mate away . . .

Today I lay all my concerns for the one I love before You, and I choose to remember who You are—the Most High, the Almighty One (v. 1). That's why I can pray now with confident hope.

Because of who You are, deliver my precious mate from harm, from evil of all kinds, from accidents, injury, and sickness. Day and night, Lord, at every moment, save my loved one (vv. 3-6).

Because of who You are, command Your angels to guard my spouse's every move, to lift him or her up, and to carry our marriage through any hard times or troubles (vv. 11-12).

You, Lord, are our true home and eternal refuge. Yes, You *will* rescue us. You have promised to protect, save, and honor us if we acknowledge who You really are—and trust You completely (vv. 14-15). And we do. We do!

May both my mate and I sleep peacefully tonight because we rest in Your trustworthy name.

Amen.

New Beginnings

My comfort in my suffering is this: Your promise preserves my life.

PSALM 119:50

Heavenly Father,

I pray today for those times when our strength seems gone, when my marriage partner and I say with the psalmist, "My heart pounds, my strength fails me; even the light has gone from my eyes" (Ps. 38:10).

Restore us, O God Almighty; make your face shine upon us, that we may be saved (Ps. 80:7).

Father, when our strength is gone, be strength for us. When we get to the end of our rope, wait for us there with Your grace—completely sufficient, free, saving, amazing (John 1:16, Eph. 1:6-7).

Restore us, O God Almighty!

When we hit the wall because of concealed disobedience to You, show us the riches of mercy and freedom to be found in You through confession and restoration (Prov. 28:13).

When we fall because we have pridefully trusted in our own wisdom or strength, help us reach out in trust to You again (Prov. 3:5-6).

Restore us, O God Almighty!

And when You choose to take one or both of us through a time of intense discipline, may we receive it as a painful-but-priceless gift from the hand of a loving father (Heb. 12:10).

I, the Lord your God, am with you. I will save you with my mighty power. I will take great delight in you, and I will quiet you with My love. I will restore your soul (from Zeph. 3:17, Ps. 23:3).

Thank You, Lord, for all the new beginnings You promise.

Amen.

Jars of Clay

We have this treasure in jars of clay to show that this all-surpassing power is from God and not from us.

2 CORINTHIANS 4:7

PRAYING FROM 2 CORINTHIANS 4

Lord and Maker,

This is our greatest treasure in life: knowing You and having Your power and love within us. We are like plain jars of clay filled with this magnificent treasure.

Today I'm aware of how fragile and fallible we are. And yet You not only reveal Yourself in spite of our cracks and imperfections, You actually use our weaknesses to show off Your power in our marriage. Anyone can tell at a glance that any goodness we have is not really coming from us but from You! Please mold us, Lord, and make our marriage into a vessel You can use, no matter how chipped or ordinary (v. 7).

We often feel hard pressed on every side of life, Lord. But because You live in us, no outside pressure can crush us. And because You are our hope, we won't ever be broken by despair (v. 8). When trials come, we know You won't abandon us. And though we may stumble and fall, we know that nothing can destroy us or our marriage (v. 9).

Continue to fill us with the treasure of Your love and power, dear Lord. We want to be Your jars of clay. Change us through the daily pressures of married life into people who reflect Your great and eternal glory.

Amen.

The Encourager

*May our Lord Jesus Christ himself and God our Father, who loved us
and by his grace gave us eternal encouragement and good hope,
encourage your hearts and strengthen you in every good deed and word.*

2 THESSALONIANS 2:16-17

Heavenly Father,

I open my heart to receive Your encouragement today—those eternal reassurances You have won for me in heaven and those daily comforts You
whisper in my spirit. Truly, You are the God of all comfort (2 Cor. 1:3).

Help me to express Your healing encouragement in my marriage
today, Lord. I don't want to weigh down my mate with anxiety or criticism but lift up with kindness and good cheer (Prov. 12:25). May my
words be like good food for my partner's spirit today, especially when
my support is needed (Rom. 15:1). Remind me to say things like:
"Everything's going to be okay," "You've come further than you give
yourself credit for," "I love you just the way you are," "I believe in you,
Babe."

Let me be as quick to list my partner's good traits—and to do so
publicly—as Paul was to compliment believers in his letters (Rom.
16:1-16, 2 Cor. 7:4-7). May this be said of me: "Here is a person who
is always encouraging and comforting, always gently urging me to live a
worthy life" (from 1 Thess. 2:12).

Father, as Your appointed encourager in my own marriage today, let
me be like the prophet Isaiah, who was blessed with "an instructed
tongue, to know the word that sustains the weary" (Isa. 50:4).

Amen.

A Blessing for Hope

ay Jesus Christ himself, who loves you and who has already given you eternal hope, also give you encouragement today.

As He fills your heart with hope, may He strengthen you for a day of goodness and unexpected blessings!

FROM 2 THESSALONIANS 2:16-17

Foxes

Catch for us the foxes, the little foxes that ruin the vineyards, our vineyards that are in bloom.

Lord,

So many blessings have already come to us by Your generous hand— You are the source of every completely satisfying gift (James 1:17). But even in our vineyard of love, little foxes can enter to ruin and steal the good things You are giving us. Our prayer today is that You will empower us to be smart enough to know that "every good and perfect gift" is worth cherishing and guarding.

These are some of the grapes of love we are most thankful for today: intimate friendship, security and comfort, home and children, and passion. Lord, open our eyes to see the sneaky foxes that might steal these bounties from the vineyard of our marriage:

—busyness or worry: "You are worried and upset about many things, but only one thing is needed" (Luke 10:41-42).

—compromises in thought or deed: "Marriage should be honored by all, and the marriage bed kept pure" (Heb. 13:4).

—pride: "When pride comes, then comes disgrace" (Prov. 11:2).

—arguing and strife: "Better a dry crust with peace and quiet than a house full of feasting, with strife" (Prov. 17:1).

—pessimistic outlook: "Hope deferred makes the heart sick" (Prov. 13:12).

Lord of this vineyard, help us to see with the eyes of the Spirit today, to guard as a high priority what You have blessed us with in our marriage.

Thank You for surrounding us today with the shield of Your favor and protection (Ps. 5:12).

In Your name we pray. Amen.

Not Tonight, Honey

I have taken off my robe—must I put it on again? I have washed my feet—must I soil them again? . . . I opened for my lover, but my lover had left; he was gone. My heart sank at his departure.

SONG OF SONGS 5:3,6

A WIFE'S PRAYER

Lord of love,

How well I understand this lover's lament! Sometimes my husband approaches me with passion in his eyes at inconvenient moments. But I feel hassled instead of wooed. I am sleepy, distracted, or irritable. And rather than rushing to receive him, I delay. Sometimes my husband goes away disappointed.

Lord, Your Word tells me that my body doesn't belong only to me but is meant to be shared with my husband (1 Cor. 7:4). "My lover is mine and I am his" (Song of Songs 2:16).

Today I pray that You would help me to be continually sensitive to my husband's advances. Let me welcome them with gladness—not rejection! And when I'm not able—physically or emotionally—to make love, help me to remember how vulnerable he is at these moments. May I keep learning new ways to reassure my husband of my great affection and desire for him.

Keep us from misunderstandings or hurt in this area, Lord. Help us to be patient when one of us must wait for the fullness of passion to awaken in the other (Song of Songs 2:7). May we both say with joy, "I belong to my lover, and his desire is for me" (Song of Songs 7:10).

Amen.

No Hint

Among you there must not be even a hint of sexual immorality, or of any kind of impurity, or of greed, because these are improper for God's holy people.

A HUSBAND'S PRAYER

Heavenly Father,
Thank You that when Christ entered my life, I became a new being (2 Cor. 5:17). Help me, Father, to express this newness in sexual fidelity in my marriage.

How much I want to be faithful to my wife—in heart, mind, and body! With Paul, I want to set the standard high—so high that there's "no hint" of immorality. No selfish liberties. No lingering thoughts or fantasies. No tolerance for jokes, innuendoes, or behaviors that show disrespect for my wife or my marriage (Eph. 5:4).

Hear my husband-prayer today: Out of reverence for You, my Lord, and because of my deep affection for the wife I treasure, I ask You to help me every day:

To choose fidelity—"Marriage should be honored by all, and the marriage bed kept pure, for God will judge the adulterer and all the sexually immoral" (Heb. 13:4).

To choose faithfulness and love—"But you, the man of God, . . . set your heart on integrity, true piety, faithfulness, love, endurance and gentleness. Fight the worthwhile battle of the faith" (1 Tim. 6:11-12, PH).

To choose wisdom—"Food gained by fraud tastes sweet to a man, but he ends up with a mouth full of gravel," and "Can a man scoop fire into his lap without his clothes being burned?" (Prov. 20:17, 6:27).

To choose pure pleasure—"Rejoice in the wife of your youth. A loving doe, a graceful deer—may her breasts satisfy you always, may you ever be captivated by her love" (Prov. 5:18-19).

Thank You that I can pursue a "no hint" marriage with confidence and joy because Your Spirit strengthens and renews me (Rom. 8:6-11) and because You are ready to forgive my shortcomings with Your mercies (1 John 1:9).

Search me, O Lord, and bring to light any compromises of sexual integrity that You find. Forgive my hidden faults; break any power they might have over me. Purify me from everything that contaminates body and spirit. Lord, I want to please You and build a marriage on what will last (2 Cor. 7:1, Ps. 19:12-14, 139:23-24).

Thank You for giving me a wife who makes my commitment to faithfulness a privilege, not a burden. Thank You for Your promise that "he who pursues righteousness and love finds life, prosperity and honor" (Prov. 21:21).

In Your powerful name I pray. Amen.

Late Again

*Jesus loved Martha and her sister and Lazarus. Yet when he heard that
Lazarus was sick, he stayed where he was two more days.*

JOHN 11:5-6

Dear Lord Jesus,

Why do You wait to rescue the ones You love? You let Lazarus struggle
and suffer through to his last breath. You let Martha and Mary watch
him die even though they were home and family to You when You had
none. They counted on You—and You didn't come.

It happened so God could be glorified (from v. 4).

What does God's glory mean, Lord Jesus, when the ones we love
face illness and death—and You don't come?

When you see My acts firsthand, you will understand and trust Me
(from vv. 11,15).

If You came, so many trials, so many irresolvable struggles, so much
heartbreak would never happen. Lord, in our marriage today we need
You. Are You coming?

*I am the resurrection and the life. Even in death, I bring new life. Do
you believe?* (from vv. 25-26).

Yes, Lord, we believe You are God. To You there is no beginning and
no end. Yet we are stuck in time, and we're afraid of painful endings.

*If you believe, you will see God's splendor revealed, and others will
come to salvation* (from vv. 40-42).

Yes, Lord, we do believe. We believe that You are already here. We
trust that You have compassion on us and share our pain. And, Lord,
we are humbled by Your tears (John 11:35).

Amen.

Heaps of Rubble

What are those feeble Jews doing? Will they restore their wall? . . . Can they bring the stones back to life from those heaps of rubble?

NEHEMIAH 4:2

Lord of heaven,

Today I'm acutely aware of deeply hurtful attitudes, words, and actions that have caused damage in my home. Like the Jews returning from Babylon, I stand before You today with broken walls all around me and ask You to bring these stones back to life. "Forgive all our sins and receive us graciously," O Lord (Hos. 14:2).

We are Your people. Any rubble in this marriage is the result of our own mistakes, yet You are "compassionate and gracious, slow to anger, abounding in love" (Ps. 103:8). Empower us with the courage of Nehemiah, who determined to rebuild Jerusalem (Neh. 2:17). Give us the sword of Your Spirit to defend us as we reinvest in our relationship (Neh. 4:19-23), and bless us with a song in our hearts.

We trust that in Your time, You will bestow on us a crown of beauty instead of these ashes (Isa. 61:3). You are a merciful God who promises new things in the midst of old (Isa. 42:9). You heal life's deepest hurts (Jer. 17:14).

Thank You, Lord! Today we claim Your promises of renewal for us and for so many husbands and wives who could say with the Israelites, "All that we treasured lies in ruins" (Isa. 64:11). We repent of the damage we've done to our union, and we promise to do the work of renewal until our marriage again shines with Your glory.

Amen.

An Apple a Day

Like an apple tree among the trees of the forest is my lover among the young men. I delight to sit in his shade, and his fruit is sweet to my taste. . . . Refresh me with apples, for I am faint with love.

SONG OF SONGS 2:3,5

Dear Lord,

I pray today for a truly bountiful life that produces the good fruits of Your Spirit in my marriage as naturally as a well-tended orchard.

The fruit of the righteous is a tree of life (Prov. 11:30).

I confess, Lord, that my first impulse is not to *bear* fruit but to eat it bite by luscious bite—to simply enjoy the pleasure of having my mate bear fruit. Help me, Lord of greedy apple eaters.

Blessed is the man who trusts in the LORD. . . . He will be like a tree planted by the water that sends out its roots by the stream . . . and never fails to bear fruit (Jer. 17:7-8).

Lord, I want to trust You. I want to become that spreading apple tree loaded with fruit today. I want my mate to feel secure in my love and find refreshment in my affection and attention. But I am so weak.

No branch can bear fruit by itself. . . . Neither can you bear fruit unless you remain in me (John 15:4).

What fruit can I give my spouse today, Lord of the orchard?

The fruit of the Spirit is love, joy, peace, patience, kindness, goodness, faithfulness, gentleness and self-control (Gal. 5:22).

Yes, Lord, fill me with Your Spirit so that I bear bushels of ripened goodness in my home. Or even one beautiful apple for my love.

Amen.

We Stand in Awe

Guard your steps when you go to the house of God. Go near to listen rather than to offer the sacrifice of fools. . . . Many words are meaningless. Therefore stand in awe of God.

ECCLESIASTES 5:1,7

O God in heaven,
We stand in awe of You today.

We live in a world of rush and clutter and misunderstandings and returned checks, but You reign in eternal splendor. Your throne is surrounded at every moment by angels singing, "Holy, holy, holy is the Lord God Almighty. . . . You are worthy, our Lord and God, to receive glory and honor and power" (Rev. 4:8,11).

Today we want to join with the angels—to worship You with listening hearts, with sincere praises, with attitudes of wonder and amazement—for You *are* worthy! In our hearts You are set apart as Lord and God (1 Pet. 3:15). Our marriage is Your rightful domain. Our wedding vows resound always in Your presence, and our love finds its fullest expression in union with You. We worship Your name today!

Forgive us, Father, for the easy familiarity, the casual disrespect and presumption, the spiritual laziness we display in Your presence. Forgive us for our long-winded speeches to You—only scraps of which we will ever remember or act on (Matt. 6:7). Today we long to be clothed instead with surrender, purity, and devotion.

For You are worthy to be exalted. And we stand in awe of You. Amen.

Beloved Enemy

See, I am sending an angel ahead of you to guard you along the way and to bring you to the place I have prepared. . . . If you listen carefully to what he says and do all that I say, I will be an enemy to your enemies and will oppose those who oppose you.

O Lord,

This I know, that You are *for* us! (Ps. 56:9). You are the stronghold of our life—of whom shall we be afraid (Ps. 27:1)? Your angel always travels with those who fear You—he sets up camp around us and delivers us from every danger (Ps. 34:7). We exalt You and thank You, great God of power!

Be a mighty enemy to every enemy of our marriage today. You know each one, Lord, when we do not. You see everything that opposes us— financially, physically, emotionally, socially, spiritually. You see the little rocks we stub our toes on. You see the huge, immovable obstacles we struggle against. And You know about each arrow that Satan aims our way.

O Lord, oppose every influence in our lives that opposes us! "May they be like chaff before the wind, with the angel of the LORD driving them away; may their path be dark and slippery, with the angel of the LORD pursuing them" (Ps. 35:5).

Our hearts' desire in this journey of our marriage is to come to the place You have already prepared for us (Exod. 23:20). It is a place of abundance, security, and delight in Your presence (Ps. 66:12; 16:5,11). Help us get there by Your saving power, Beloved Enemy!

Amen.

Mind on a Diet

Whatever is true, whatever is noble, whatever is right, whatever is pure,
whatever is lovely, whatever is admirable—if anything is excellent or
praiseworthy—think about such things.

PHILIPPIANS 4:8

Dear Lord Jesus,

I know my spouse so well! I confess I am able to list for You my mate's
faults, explaining in great detail and with sincere concern just how You,
all-knowing Lord, should step in to fix them. How sad that the famili-
arities of marriage get turned into weapons to hurt, reasons to hedge on
commitments, or excuses to remain distant or bitter.

Today, Lord, I plead with You to cleanse my mind of critical or
unloving thoughts. I release them now to You. Let me see my marriage
partner with the mind of Christ (1 Cor. 2:12-16). When You, Savior,
looked on a broken, hateful world, You saw only reasons to die so that
we might live (Luke 19:10, Rom. 5:8).

Yes, Lord, whatever is excellent or praiseworthy in each other, let
these thoughts fill our minds. Reveal to us what is pure in the other's
motives, what is noble and true in the other's character, what is lovely
in our partner's personality, what is admirable about our spouse's efforts,
and what our mate accomplishes each day that is excellent and praiseworthy.

Help both of us to grasp and enjoy every evidence of God at work
in us. May we clearly see and celebrate these qualities—and be blind to
all the rest.

Amen.

When You Know Too Much

The knowledge of where people are wrong is a hindrance to prayer, not an assistance. "I want to tell you of the difficulties so that you may pray intelligently." The more you know the less intelligently you pray because you forget to believe that God can alter the difficulties.

OSWALD CHAMBERS

Turn Our Hearts

Rend your heart and not your garments. Return to the LORD your God, for he is gracious and compassionate, slow to anger and abounding in love.

JOEL 2:13

Loving Lord,
No matter what day of the week it is, we can always say, "We must return to the Lord!" For we are always straying, Father. Even while we try to do right, our hearts sin (Rom. 7:15). Even now as we stop to pray, a part of us would rather do something else.

We agree with Your Word—the heart is deceitful above all things (Jer. 17:9).

Lord, we offer our hearts to You—all their bruises, numbness, and dark corners. You promised that You would turn the heart of stone into a heart of flesh (Ezek. 36:26).

Pour out Your Spirit on us, Lord. Turn our hearts to You, and toward one another, and toward all who are part of this family (Mal. 4:6).

Yes, turn our hearts. Break our hearts. And then heal our hearts, dear Lord. We are Yours!

In repentance and rest is your salvation (Isa. 30:15).
Amen.

Pressure Sensitive

*We were under great pressure, far beyond our ability to endure, so that
we despaired even of life. Indeed, in our hearts we felt the sentence of
death. But this happened that we might not rely on ourselves but on
God, who raises the dead.*

2 CORINTHIANS 1:8-9

Heavenly Father,

You know that we sometimes feel enormous pressures in our life together, forces that seem about to crush us—schedules, finances, kids in
trouble, personal conflict, obstacles at work or at church. We understand Paul when he admitted that he was pushed far beyond his ability
to endure. Specifically, we pray about these pressures from within and
without today: _____ , _____ and _____.

You are a God who saves (Ps. 68:20). Lord, save us!

You are a God who fights for us (2 Chron. 20:17). Lord, fight for us!

You are a God who intervenes (Isa. 49:24-25). Lord, intervene with
one of Your miracles!

You are the Lord of every day (Ps. 118:24), and on days when we
have no resistance left at all, You promise that the grace and strength of
Your Spirit are at their mightiest (2 Cor. 12:9)!

Help my mate and me to keep up our courage today and look for
Your deliverances. Thank You that You are sensitive to our every need
(Ps. 23:5). And thank You that even in terrible pressures we don't have
to lose heart, because Your Spirit is renewing us inwardly day by day
(2 Cor. 4:16-17).

Amen.

Habakkuk's Hope

How long, O LORD, must I call for help, but you do not listen?

PRAYING WITH THE PROPHET HABAKKUK

Dear Lord,
Today I bring before You those needs inside my marriage that don't
seem to go away. I pray specifically about _____. And I put
into Your hands as well all the pressures and difficulties that come from
outside.

How many days I've placed these concerns before You in deep need
but with genuine trust! When will You answer, Lord? I am waiting to
see what You will say to me (2:1).

Please show me if I'm ignoring any sin—of wrong things done, of
good things left undone—that might be keeping You from working in
me or me from enjoying Your holy presence (1:2).

You *are* a God who acts. I am in awe of what You've done for Your
people in the past. Please do the same miracles, or even greater ones, in
my life and my marriage (3:2).

I wait in hope with this conviction: *You are acting right now,* even
when I don't see or feel You. I will wait patiently for You today—because You ask Your people to live by faith (2:4).

With Habakkuk, I make this my testimony: "Though the fig tree
does not bud and there are no grapes on the vines, though the olive
crop fails and the fields produce no food, though there are no sheep in

the pen and no cattle in the stalls, yet I will rejoice in the LORD, I will be joyful in God my Savior. The Sovereign LORD is my strength" (3:17-19).

Amen.

Flooded with Light

I pray that your hearts will be flooded with light so that you can see something of the future he has called you to share.

EPHESIANS 1:18, TLB

Precious Lord,

Our prayer today is that You will flood our hearts with the light of Your truth. Chase away every dark shadow of distraction, protected sin, pro-crastination, or disobedience.

Lord, since the day we said "I do," the future we've been called to share together has been dear to us. But we lose sight of it so easily. We become prisoners of the now—in how we treat each other, in how we spend our time and our money and our energy, in what we think about . . .

Some days the destiny You promise just slips into shadows. But You can turn any darkness into dawn (Amos 5:8). And because we are Your dearly loved children, You ask us to imitate You and exhibit the fruit of the light—all goodness, righteousness and truth (Eph. 5:1,8-9).

Shine here, Lord! At each step, turn every dark confusion about our purposes and our future into bright light of understanding, as You've promised (Isa. 42:16). Yes, lead us—even in new and unfamiliar paths today—to bring glory to You.

Amen.

My Soul, Your Lamp

Hear us, O never-failing light, Lord our God, the fountain of light, the light of your angels, principalities, powers and of all intelligent beings; who has created the light of your saints. May our souls be lamps of yours, kindled and illuminated by you. May they shine and burn with the truth, and never go out in darkness and ashes. May the gloom of sins be cleared away, and the light of perpetual faith abide in us.

A Spanish Liturgy from the
Sixth to Eighth Century

A Salty End

As soon as they had brought them out, [an angel] said, "Flee for your lives! Don't look back, and don't stop anywhere in the plain! . . ." But Lot's wife looked back, and she became a pillar of salt.

GENESIS 19:17,26

A WIFE'S PRAYER

Lord,

Why did Lot's wife, against the advice of angels, just *have* to look back? Was she just wanting one last nostalgic look, or was she worried about something she'd left behind?

Today I pray that I will not make the same mistake. Your Word is filled with warnings about the perils of holding on to the past (Isa. 43:18), or remembering the past with foolish longing (Num. 11:5), or turning back spiritually after we belong to You (Luke 9:62).

Help me to continually fix my eyes on You, Lord. You are looking for those who will follow You unwaveringly, sure of the miraculous redemption You are guiding them toward.

Save my spouse and me! We don't want to dwell in unhealthy ways on past failures or even past successes. Show us both these pivotal moments, Lord, when looking backward would be dangerous. We want to quickly obey when You say into our spirits, "Don't look back now!"

Save us from a salty end!

Today we will look only ahead and say, "There is surely a future hope for us!" (from Prov. 23:18).

Amen.

Dangling Conversations

During the days of Jesus' life on earth, he offered up prayers and petitions with loud cries and tears to the one who could save him from death, and he was heard because of his reverent submission.

HEBREWS 5:7

A HUSBAND'S PRAYER

Dear Lord Jesus,

Hear me in this house today. Hear me on the job. Receive my faltering stops and starts, my well-intentioned but half-delivered prayers on behalf of my marriage. Let ours be a house where love is both subject and verb all day—*Love lives here; here, we love.*

I know You receive my pleadings, Lord Jesus, when they don't even sound like prayers. You prayed on mountainsides (Matt. 14:23) and in the early morning dark (Mark 1:35). You wailed. You sobbed (Heb. 5:7). But You kept on praying.

Help me to keep on praying for my wife—to begin again as many times as it takes—all day long. This is a kind of "praying continually" (1 Thess. 5:17) that I can manage—when I look at her picture, when I hear her voice on the phone, when hard feelings flare, when I think how much a part of everything that matters to me she really is.

"Help, O God . . . !" "Lord, for her I ask . . ." "Bless . . ." Let these spare parts of conversations be fitted together by Your Spirit to become eloquent and whole in Your ears (Rom. 8:26-27). You, O Lord, are the One who can save us from every harm.

Amen.

Praying the Ten Commandments

Keep his decrees and commands . . . so that it may go well with you and
your children after you.

P R A Y I N G   T H E   T E N   C O M M A N D M E N T S

Lord God,
We want to worship You in our home today by keeping Your commands foremost in our memories and affections (Deut. 6:6) and by making them part of the fabric of our married life. Show us, Lord, what it means to fear You and keep Your laws (Deut. 7:12).

1. *I am the LORD your God, who brought you out of . . . slavery. You shall have no other gods before me* (5:6-7). May no other loyalties or affections take Your place in our hearts—no other priority, hobby, ambition, possession, or person. We belong to only You!

2. *You shall not make for yourself an idol in the form of anything in heaven . . . or on earth. . . . You shall not . . . worship them; for I . . . am a jealous God* (5:8-9). Help us to resist any substitute objects of worship and to turn away from all false beliefs. Keep us from any pursuit—no matter how worthy—that becomes an end in itself.

3. *You shall not misuse the name of the LORD your God* (5:11). Help us to treasure and protect Your name, O Lord. In a casually profane world, keep us sensitive about the sacredness of Your names, especially "Lord," "God," and "Jesus Christ."

4. *Observe the Sabbath day by keeping it holy* (5:12-15). May we faithfully set aside the Lord's day for worship and rest and for nurturing

a vital role in Your church family. Thank You for setting both of us free from the tyranny of work and "getting ahead."

5. *Honor your father and your mother, as the LORD your God has commanded you, so that you may live long and that it may go well with you* (5:16). Help us to teach our children to respect and obey us as You've asked. And may we treat our own parents in exactly the same way. We will look for Your blessings as a result.

6. *You shall not murder* (5:17). Help us to understand and guard the sanctity of all human life—including the unborn or aged. May we never, even in our thoughts, surrender to hate, violence, or taking revenge.

7. *You shall not commit adultery* (5:18). Show us ways to build our marriage relationship on integrity, purity, faithfulness, and loyalty. Protect both of us from the traps of pornography or promiscuity. May we renew our commitment continually to honor our marriage as a sacred, lifelong trust.

8. *You shall not steal* (5:19). Help us to value personal honesty in little and large issues, to respect the belongings of others, and to trust You, our Provider, to take care of all our wants and needs.

9. *You shall not give false testimony against your neighbor* (5:20). Instill in us a sincere dedication to being loyal and truthful in all our relationships.

10. *You shall not covet* (5:21). Help us never to measure our happiness by the lives or possessions of others. Instead, may we be content with what You give and happy when others prosper.

Lord God, thank You for Your gracious promise to bless us and our children if we follow these laws. We want Your covenant of love to be the measure of our lives (7:12).

Amen.

Love Is Glue

Over all these virtues put on love, which binds them all together in perfect unity.

COLOSSIANS 3:14

Holy Lord of love, who with bleeding hands reached out and pulled together God's perfect heaven and my imperfect heart,

Be love in our marriage today. Hold us gently, firmly. Don't let us go (Col. 1:17).

So many forces try to pull us apart: hurry, doubt, flu and colds, distrust, squabbling kids, the remote control, familiarity, carelessness. These daily assaults try to separate us from each other and from You.

Hold us together with Your loving hands, saving Lord (Ps. 73:23). When we split, shift, and break apart, in every crack let evidences of love flourish: mercy, kindness, humility, acceptance, patience, tolerance, forgiveness (Col. 3:12-13, PH).

And help us, Lord, to cover every day with a thick, permeating, wonderfully sticky coating of love—the conspiracy of hearts to win over every obstacle, the glue of heaven that can hold us all together as You want.

Amen.

The Power of Two

The king again asked Esther, "Now what is your petition? It will be given you. And what is your request? Even up to half the kingdom, it will be granted."

ESTHER 5:6

Lord,

We come to you right now with a confession on our lips: We compete for power in our marriage. We both want to be in charge!

Hear our prayer, Lord: May the war of the sexes go down in defeat in our marriage today!

Teach us, Father, from the story of Queen Esther and King Xerxes. Though they had never read Paul's letters, they were Old Testament examples of his New Testament advice: for wives to reverence their husbands (Eph. 5:21-24), for husbands to cherish their wives like their own bodies (v. 28), and for both spouses to submit to one another in love (v. 21).

When Esther wanted to persuade her husband, she affirmed her respect for Xerxes and his position while making her request in a dignified, straightforward way. "If I have found favor with you, O king, and if it pleases your majesty, grant me my life—this is my petition. And spare my people—this is my request" (Esther 7:3).

Today we, too, want to honor each other, even when we see things differently and there's a lot at stake. Give us the wisdom to emulate Esther's gracious manner, respect, and forthrightness.

When King Xerxes could have used his power to ignore or intimidate his wife, he did the opposite. He made her concerns his own and conceded that he had made a mistake by trusting an evil man. And Xerxes continued to ask Esther how to make things right again for the Jewish people. "Now write another decree in the king's name in behalf of the Jews as seems best to you, and seal it with the king's signet ring" (8:8).

Today we, too, want to lift each other up through a willingness to surrender or share our rights and powers. Give us the grace to be as generous and wise as Xerxes when our mate needs our attention, acceptance, or help.

Lord, show us how You have given each of us power in this marriage—and that it's an opportunity to do good, not harm. Please teach us each day how to "wield" our power humbly and tenderly. For *greater* is the power of two in the kingdom of love (Eccles. 3:10-12).

Amen.

Every Rainbow Is for You

He has given us his very great and precious promises.

2 PETER 1:4

Dear heavenly Father,
Today I thank You for Your priceless promises that make our lives possible.

Thank You that You are a God of Your word (Num. 23:19). Yes, like a golden ribbon around our lives, Your pledge of kindness holds all our hopes together (Neh. 9:17-33).

Especially for my spouse today, I claim these "great and precious promises":

Never will I leave you; never will I forsake you (Heb. 13:5).

I am your provider and protector, comforter and friend (from Ps. 23:1, 27:1; Isa. 25:8; John 15:15).

If two of you on earth agree about anything you ask for, it will be done for you (Matt. 18:19).

Everyone who receives Me and believes in My name becomes a child of God (from John 1:12).

My kindness, mercies, and love for you are inexhaustible! (from Ps. 18:50, 25:6; Jer. 31:3).

O bountiful and good Father, I praise You today! I exalt Your name! And it's with deeply felt thanks that I claim Your loving promises for my marriage partner. Let each promise be a bright, colorful rainbow of encouragement and confidence on my mate's horizon.

Amen.

Heal Our Blindness

Two blind men were sitting by the roadside, and when they heard that Jesus was going by, they shouted, "Lord, Son of David, have mercy on us!"

MATTHEW 20:30

Lord, Son of David,

Today my spouse and I are sitting by the roadside with a need we can't fix. We can't even see You, Lord, but we know You will pass by. You have been here before. You have never let us down.

Lord, our Messiah; Lord, our healer; Lord Jesus, merciful Savior—we call out Your name! Hear our prayer—our exact need—when the only words that come to our lips are, "Lord, have mercy!"

Heal our blindness, Lord. We don't even know what it is we can't see—about a situation we face, about each other, about You . . .

Show us what steps toward wholeness You are asking us to take. We want with all our hearts to be part of Your miracle story in this house.

And right now we shout praise to You, Lord Jesus, because You *do* come to us in our need, as ready to heal us as You were willing to be wounded for us (Isa. 53:5). With the psalmist we will tell everyone: "I love the LORD, for he heard my voice; he heard my cry for mercy. Because he turned his ear to me, I will call on him as long as I live" (Ps. 116:1-2).

And we will rise from this dust to follow You.

Amen.

Break Down the Strongholds

It is for freedom that Christ has set us free. Stand firm, then, and do not let yourselves be burdened again by a yoke of slavery.

GALATIANS 5:1

Lord Jesus Christ,

I pray today that my precious life partner will be released from any spiritual powers that may be holding him or her captive.

I don't pray with any power of my own; only You are our Savior and liberator (1 John 4:14). Only You are greater than Satan or any authority or influence in this world (1 John 4:4, Jude 9). You have disarmed all the powers of evil and "made a public spectacle of them, triumphing over them by the cross" (Col. 2:15). And You are stronger than any addiction, habit, dependency, or destructive pull in my spouse's life (Ps. 103:3-4).

I exalt and honor You, victorious Lord (1 Cor. 15:25-27)!

In Your name and by the power of Your costly shed blood, please rescue _____ and bring my dear mate into Your kingdom of light (Phil. 2:9-11, Heb. 9:11-14, Col. 1:13)!

Especially break down the strongholds that my loved one can't see—dungeon doors like bitterness, spiritual blindness, immorality, or fear (2 Cor. 10:3-4, Heb. 12:15, 2 Cor. 4:4, 1 Cor. 6:9-10, Rom. 8:15). And keep this precious one from thoughtlessly sliding back again into bondage (Gal. 5:1,19-21). We want to be Your redeemed people (Titus 2:14).

I thank You and worship You right now in faith for the deliverances and new beginnings You have brought, are bringing, and will yet bring, Lord Jesus!

And as You deliver us, take up residence wholly in us, filling every corner of our lives (Luke 11:21-26). Where there used to be sin, may Your Holy Spirit bring the beautiful fruit of love, joy, peace, patience, kindness, goodness, gentleness, and self-control (Gal. 5:22).

Awesome Lord, because You have called us to freedom, my life partner, _____, is free *indeed* (John 8:36)!

Amen.

A Blessing for Freedom

n Jesus' name, I bless you for a day of freedom. May His truth release you from whatever tries to hold you captive today—because you know the truth "and the truth will set you free."

FROM JOHN 8:32

Lord of the Way

I will instruct you and teach you in the way you should go; I will counsel you and watch over you.

PSALM 32:8

Lord,

I pray today for You to open the way ahead of us. We can't make the right decisions without You. How blessed we are to have the Lord of the universe as our companion and guide. You are "the Lord Almighty, wonderful in counsel and magnificent in wisdom" (Isa. 28:29). In my relationship with my spouse, I pray for specific direction about _____. And for the needs of our home today, I pray specifically about _____. All day, Lord, I will listen for Your counsel, however it might come to me (Isa. 30:21).

Yes, be our guide. As we use the abilities and information we have, nudge us in the right direction. When we get lost because of ignorance or wrong motives, mercifully intervene. You are the Lord of each choice (Prov. 16:9).

We have traveled many unfamiliar roads in our life together—and arrived at completely unexpected destinations because You have guided us. In the wilderness You've made a path. In the dark You've switched on the light. And You have never forsaken us (Isa. 42:16).

We have every reason to trust You! Thank You, Lord.

Today, may Your joy and peace flow through us even when we feel lost (Isa. 55:12). And may our quiet, hope-filled attitudes flow back to You as gifts of sincere worship (Isa. 30:15).

Thank You, Lord of the way ahead.

Amen.

Changed by Love

God has made us what we are, created in Christ Jesus to do those good deeds which he planned for us to do.

EPHESIANS 2:10, PH

PRAYING WITH PAUL

Dear heavenly Father,

I fall on my knees before You and pray that through Your unlimited resources You will enable my dear spouse to know the strength of the Spirit's inner reinforcement—that Christ may actually live in his or her heart today by faith (Eph. 3:14-16).

And I pray that my mate, firmly secure in the daily love we share, will experience a continually greater understanding of how wide and deep and long and high is the eternal love of Christ! May my precious one encounter that love personally and be changed by it—even though this love seems so far beyond our comprehension (vv. 17-19).

Yes, may my spouse's being be filled with God himself (v. 19).

Now to You, heavenly Father, who by Your power within us are able to do infinitely more than we ever dare to ask or imagine—to You alone be glory in our marriage. Always (vv. 20-21).

Amen.

The Upside–Down Kingdom

*He got up from the meal, took off his outer clothing, and wrapped a
towel around his waist. After that, he poured water into a basin and
began to wash his disciples' feet.*

JOHN 13:4-5

Dear Lord Jesus,
So often You ask us to do the opposite of what comes naturally. We
want to hate, but You say love. We want to run, but You say stay. We
want to take, but You say give.

And Your life proved every word You preached!

Open our eyes, amazing Lord, to the life-giving truths of Your
upside-down kingdom. We want to be Your faithful disciples.

If anyone wants to first, he must be the very last, and the servant of all
(Mark 9:35).

Motivate my spouse and me to serve each other first, putting our
own needs on hold for a time if we must. Help us to be "first" to initi-
ate a healing talk, clean up a mess, make the call, shower with compliments.

Whoever loses his life for me and for the gospel will save it (Mark
8:35).

The lure of self-centeredness in our world is so strong. But lead us
toward the greater attraction of sacrificing our own petty plans for Your
eternally significant purposes. May we feel most possessive of being
possessed by You.

Love your enemies and pray for those who persecute you (Matt.
5:44).

Help us to remember that it is hurt, fear, or need that so often explains the meanness of others. Prompt us to pray for those who treat us badly—and bless us with Your amazing peace as a result.

By Your Spirit powerfully at work in our home, help us to be walking, talking proofs of Your upside-down gospel.

In Your name we pray. Amen.

A Blessing for God's People

The LORD bless you and keep you; the LORD make his face shine upon you and be gracious to you; the LORD turn his face toward you and give you peace.

NUMBERS 6:24-26

Our Pilgrim Family

Blessed are those who dwell in your house; they are ever praising you.
Blessed are those whose strength is in you, who have set their hearts on
pilgrimage.

PSALM 84:4-5

Heavenly Father,

Our prayers today rise up from the road, from among our traveling
companions. We acknowledge that we are spiritual sojourners—we
don't belong to the material world we see but are citizens of another
kingdom, an eternal one (Phil. 3:20). Our mortgages and car payments
are only tent pegs—our hearts are set on pilgrimage!

Today we worship and thank You for our pilgrim family, Your
church. We're so grateful, Father, for the believers You bring alongside
to mentor and encourage us, to be Your face and hands in our times of
need. Thank You that we are among "the people of God"— chosen,
royal, holy, belonging to You. May we flourish in the company of Your
"household" (Ps. 101:6, 1 Tim. 3:15, 1 Pet. 2:9).

Give us a deep passion for and a commitment to Your church, the
bride of Christ on earth. May we be willing, as Christ was, to live sacrificially for it and protect its reputation in the world, especially among
nonbelievers (1 Cor. 10:31, 1 Thess. 4:9-12). May we be faithful in our
worship, giving, and serving (Heb. 10:25).

Be with Your family today, Lord, as we journey together toward the
place Your Son is preparing for us all (John 14:2).

Amen.

Soft Words

A soft answer turns away wrath, but harsh words cause quarrels.

PROVERBS 15:1, TLB

Lord,
Touch my words with softness today—and touch the thoughts and impulses behind the words, and the motives behind those.

Let every word and tone of voice be like a gentle rain of kindness today on the thirsty heart of my beloved (Prov. 16:15).

With soft words of affirmation—not quick words of criticism—let me fill my mate's life with good things (Prov. 12:14).

With soft words of discretion and patience—not reckless words that pierce like a sword—let me be a wise partner who brings healing (Prov. 12:18).

With soft words of compassion—not careless gossip or slander—bless our marriage with a long life and more happiness than we can imagine (Ps. 34:12-14).

With soft words of kindness—not sarcastic or cutting remarks—help us to wash away all bitterness, anger, upset, and hurtfulness (Eph. 4:31-32).

With soft words of respect—not defensiveness or self-righteousness—may every conversation be gentle, full of mercy, and truly courteous (Titus 3:2, TLB).

You are the meek and gentle Savior who can change even big mouths like me. By Your soft words of life, bring our marriage hope and love today.

Amen.

When the Story Stops

O Lord, where is your former great love, which in your faithfulness you swore to David?

PSALM 89:49

Lord,

Sometimes Your presence in our marriage suddenly seems to have disappeared. We don't see evidence of the growth that we'd hoped for by now, and sometimes we wonder aloud, "Will God ever come back again to bless us?" (from Ps. 77:7).

At these times when Your story of love seems to have stopped here, help us trust the evidence. Your past goodness is all around us! Yes, we see Your blessing in our children's faces, in our daily bread and good health, in answered prayers (Ps. 128:1-4). Let these evidences speak loudly when You do not, Lord. Help us remember that our wavering feelings don't change the truth of Your unwavering love (Ps. 103:17, 2 Tim. 2:13).

Today I choose to say with the psalmist: "I will remember the deeds of the LORD. You are the God who performs miracles; with your mighty arm you redeemed your people. Your path led through the sea, your way through the mighty waters, though your footprints were not seen" (from Ps. 77:11-19).

We will trust that Your love story in our home is still being told. You will fulfill Your purpose for us. Your love, O Lord, for us will *never* stop! You will never abandon the "story" You have started here (Ps. 138:8).

Amen.

Love Is Not Blind

o love another is to will what is really good for him. Such love must be based on truth. A love that sees no distinction between good and evil, but loves blindly merely for the sake of loving, is hatred, rather than love. To love blindly is to love selfishly, because the goal of such love is not the real advantage of the beloved but only the exercise of love in our own soul.

THOMAS MERTON

The Rebuke of a Friend

If a Christian is overcome by some sin, you who are godly should gently and humbly help him back onto the right path, remembering that next time it might be one of you who is in the wrong.

GALATIANS 6:1, TLB

Heavenly Father,

I have to confess, talking honestly with my spouse about a wrong behavior or attitude is not on my list of favorite things to do. Who am I to judge? And won't it just tear us apart?

God, who reconciled us to himself through Christ, gave us the ministry of reconciliation (2 Cor. 5:18). *Wounds from a friend can be trusted* (Prov. 27:6).

Yes, Lord, that's the point—I don't want to inflict wounds! Can't I simply pray and hope this problem will go away? Wouldn't that be more loving?

Better is open rebuke than hidden love (Prov. 27:5). *Love does not delight in evil but rejoices with the truth* (1 Cor. 13:6).

Lord, season my honesty with sensitivity and affection (Eph. 4:15). Temper my words with mercy. Please search my heart right now. Show me if there's any area where I, too, need correction (Ps. 139:23-24). May I never be prideful but as open to my spouse's candid feedback as I want my spouse to be to mine.

Help us to work through any anger, disappointment, or defensiveness and arrive together at a godly sorrow that honors You and leads to change for the better (2 Cor. 7:10).

Amen.

Good Problems

When all kinds of trials and temptations crowd into your lives, my brothers, don't resent them as intruders, but welcome them as friends! Realise that they come to test your faith and to produce in you the quality of endurance. But let the process go on until that endurance is fully developed, and you will find you have become men of mature character.

JAMES 1:2-4, PH

O heavenly Father,

How difficult it is for our family to welcome trials and temptations as friends. And the difficulties we face are nothing like the persecution and violence faced by the early Christians to whom James was writing.

Father, please give us that radical, first-century faith that could find a reason to relish problems. You are so often at work in our trials; in fact, the problems we face are often Your "solutions":

—In our stress today, You're giving us an opportunity to learn patience (James 1:3).

—In our doubts, You are inviting us to develop a trial-tested faith that pleases You (Heb. 11:6).

—In our failures and embarrassments, You want to teach us humility (James 4:6).

Today, Lord, we humbly give You permission to hold off any solution long enough to force us to grow through the problem. Only grant us Your joy, peace, and strength in the process. Your Word promises that all who surrender their problems (and solutions) to You are blessed (Isa. 30:18). Thank You!

In Jesus' name. Amen.

Hope in Him

Find rest, O my soul, in God alone; my hope comes from him.

PSALM 62:5

MEDITATION PRAYERS FOR HOPE

Lord,

When we're discouraged, it's so easy to put our hope in the next pay raise, the next vacation, a new car . . .

Today we put all of our hope in You. We will speak Your words to our souls, and we will meditate on them all day long.

> We wait in hope for the LORD;
> he is our help and our shield.
> In him our hearts rejoice,
> for we trust in his holy name.
> (Ps. 33:20-21)

> Why are you downcast, O my soul? . . .
> Put your hope in God,
> for I will yet praise him.
> (Ps. 42:11)

> May your unfailing love rest upon us,
> O LORD,
> even as we put our hope in you.
> (Ps. 33:22)

House Rules

Every city or household divided against itself will not stand.

MATTHEW 12:25

Lord of peace,
You say it is good, pleasant, and profitable for families to live together in harmony (Ps. 133:1-3). Lord, let our house rule be "to build each other up, to stand together, to love as one." Two people can't even walk down the road together unless they're going in the same direction (Amos 3:3). How much more for us who are married?

Your Word encourages us to "live together in harmony, live together in love, as though you had only one mind and one spirit between you" (Phil. 2:2, PH). May our family be like the first Christians who were so changed by their new faith that they seemed to share one heart (Acts 4:32).

Help us, O Lord of peace!

Help us watch what we say to each other—nothing divisive or deceitful—so that Your goodness can fill our lives (Ps. 34:12-14).

Help us watch how we treat each other. Give us a determination to pick up the instruments of peace—pure motives, considerateness, submission, fairness, mercy, and love (James 3:17). It's our sincere desire, Lord, to "accept life with humility and patience, generously making allowances for each other" (Eph. 4:2, PH).

Breathe into our home Your powerful Spirit of unity today so that we live out our "house rules" in a way that pleases You (Rom. 15:5). With one clear voice, may our marriage lift up Your name and show the world that You are real (John 17:23).

Amen.

True Love

And now I will show you the most excellent way.

PRAYING 1 CORINTHIANS 13 (A WIFE'S PRAYER)

Dear Lord,
What would You like to say to me today? I am listening.

If you speak in the tongues of humans and of angels . . .

Wait a minute, Lord. I'm tired of this chapter. I know it by heart.

. . . but don't communicate love to your husband in a way he under-stands, you are only a nagging nuisance, an irritating noise.

Well, okay. I do nag now and then . . .

If you give all you can to him—pick up his socks, make his favorite dinners, give your energy to make his dreams come true—

That's it, Lord. I give and give to this marriage—and I hardly re-member who am I or what I wanted . . .

. . . but he doesn't feel loved by you, you aren't accomplishing anything.

Now wait, Lord. I said I give almost everything for him. That should count for something.

Love is patient; love is kind.

But that's not always possible! He's so completely, frustratingly . . . male! He gets glued all weekend to TV sports. Or he disap-pears into the garage. I wish I had that kind of luxury. I wish *I* had a wife . . .

Love doesn't envy or boast.

You're right, Lord. I'm not better than he is. And I have my own ideas about fun and relaxation.

Love doesn't put its own needs first.

Lord, I do want to serve and honor my husband—even when his needs are directly opposite of mine. Help me to remember that when I'm willing to meet his needs first, he's usually eager to serve me too. Help me see the big picture when it doesn't seem to be working out that way and my blood pressure starts to rise.

Love doesn't get angry or keep score.

Yes, Lord! Help me to stop trying to remake my guy into some perfect husband that doesn't even exist. Help me to put away my time clock and my scorepad.

Love ignores mistakes and faults and rejoices in the important truths.

This is what's important: He loves me. He tries hard. He comes home every night. He cares about our family. He wants to do what's right. He wants to honor You . . .

Love always works hard to believe the best, to trust the motives of others.

You've given me a good man, Lord. Give me Your strength to love him well—to believe in his good intentions and to trust what You're doing in his life.

Thank You, Father, for this husband of mine.

Love never gives up or gives out.

Please give me many more years of Monday night football with the man I love. May we always bless each with Your "most excellent way."

Amen.

Swept Away

May your roots go down deep into the soil of God's marvelous love; and may you be able to feel and understand, as all God's children should, how long, how wide, how deep, and how high his love really is; and to experience this love for yourselves.

EPHESIANS 3:17-19, TLB

A HUSBAND'S PRAYER

Dear Lord of love,

You are the One who pursues us day and night. You know my wife and me perfectly. You surround us with Your loving care like a warm blanket, like a wall of protection, like an ocean of mercy (Ps. 139:1-10). The earth is full of it! The skies can't contain it (Ps. 119:64, 103:11)!

My prayer today is that my wife will know Your love—really take it in—in a fresh way. So much about even the best human love is incomplete, tarnished, and unreliable. But Your love, O God, is perfect and complete.

May my wife be swept away all day by the wonder of Your love. When she hears You say, "I love you, _____!" may she begin to grasp how much!

—so much that You chose her as a worthy object of Your devoted affection and commitment (Ezek. 16:8);

—so much that You promised her Your love "unto death" before she deserved it, asked for it, or even knew about it (Rom. 5:8, Isa. 53:12);

—so much that You have brought her into Your family (1 John 3:1) and saved her from perishing eternally (John 3:16);

—so much that You cover her every day with love and compassion (Ps. 103:4);

—so much that when she is in distress, You are in distress too (Isa. 63:9);

—so much that You are willing to gently chasten and redirect her when she strays (Heb. 12:6);

—so much that You protect the relationship You share with a veil of continuing forgiveness—You have put all her past, present, and future offenses to You behind Your back (Isa. 38:17);

—so much that You enrich her mind and imagination with the insights of Your Spirit, You bless her body with healing and strength, and You flood her innermost being with a sense of Your acceptance (Ps. 146:8);

—so much that she can go through her whole life knowing that God's love for her is true (John 16:27), unfailing (Ps. 147:11), and never ending (Jer. 31:3)!

O God of love, hear this husband's prayer today. Bless my dear wife with a deeper, wider, and higher assurance of Your incredible love for her than she has ever experienced before.

And I pray for this miracle too: "Complete" Your love in the love I demonstrate to her today (1 John 4:12). Yes, You can accomplish this miracle, Lord, because You *are* love (1 John 4:16)—and our marriage is just another ray of Your amazing love story shining in this world.

Amen.

Christ in Us

And this is the secret: that Christ in your hearts is your only hope of glory.

PRAYING FROM COLOSSIANS

Dear heavenly Father,

We may have great kids, sincere love, and money in the bank, but apart from Christ's presence and power, we are a couple without hope.

Thank You, wonderful Father, that we *do* possess hope! We know the secret to life—that Jesus Christ *is* God and He lives in us (1:27). Yes, *Christ in us!* Through Your Son, You have given us new life and a forever hope (2:13).

How blessed we are to remember that when You look at each of us—before we've even had coffee or brushed our teeth, and we can only mumble "Mornin' . . ."—You see the shining beauty of Christ in us (3:3). Thank You, Father!

Fill our relationship with Your hope and peace today (3:15). Let the Spirit of Christ so blossom in our lives (3:16) that when we come to the end of our own resources, we can remember to find strength in our family's greatest secret: *Christ in us!*

During a hard moment on the job, when we're stuck in a traffic jam, when a child hates what's for dinner—*Christ in us! Christ in us! Christ in us* (3:16)!

Thank You for our family's secret, Father. Today we want to share it with others, even declare it boldly, to anyone who will listen.

Amen.

Stuck in a Rut

But I trust in you, O LORD; I say, "You are my God." My times are in your hands.

PSALM 31:14-15

Dear Lord,

I'm afraid we've become one of *those* couples we vowed we'd never be: same conversations, same laundry, same store aisles, same commute, same clutter, same face across the table.

We didn't see it coming, this rut we've fallen into. It's like each day's routines have created a groove that has worn deeper with each passing year.

Forgive us if we're being shortsighted or selfish, Lord. Help us to humbly accept the realities of being human. Open our eyes to see that even in the deep grooves of ordinary life, You—most amazing God!—are always up to something exciting and miraculous (Isa. 43:18-19, Job 38:4–39:30).

By Your grace, help us to see Your steadfast love in every routine. And when sameness seems to close in on us, help us to reach for You in trust. You *are* at work in both sameness and change (James 1:17-18).

Today, Lord, we gladly respond to Your exciting invitation to be like You—*redundantly faithful all over again each day* (Rev. 2:10).

Amen.

Three Times Always

Be joyful always; pray continually; give thanks in all circumstances, for this is God's will for you in Christ Jesus.

1 THESSALONIANS 5:16-18

Heavenly Father,

In this verse You have showed me Your desire for me and for my marriage today. By Your power working in me, help me to live out these commitments in practical ways:

I will be joyful always—When she burns my favorite dinner, when he still hasn't fixed the screen door, when we are at cross-purposes, when our money runs out . . . at *all* times, I will rest in the contentment and optimism that is mine through Christ (Phil. 4:4-13,19). Joy is Your gift to me, Lord (Isa. 12:3). And today I choose to rejoice in my marriage and in every other circumstance (Phil. 4:4).

I will pray always—In hush or in hullabaloo, in our boredom or in our busyness, in moments of tension or of peace, I will keep an on-going spiritual conversation with You. Thank You, God, for the mysterious privilege of abiding *always* in constant relationship with You (John 15:1-8). Prayer is Your gift to me, Lord (Jer. 33:3), and a day full of prayer that pervades my marriage and every other activity is my gift back to You (Ps. 27:8).

I will be thankful always—even when we fail at something that really matters to us, or when everything seems to be going against us, or when one of us lets the other down, or when Your answers are slow in coming. Thank You, God, that thankfulness *in everything* is a realistic and freeing way of life for Your children (Eph. 5:20). I choose it today. And I worship You with my whole heart.

Amen.

Called and Bound

e sin against the Lord when we stop praying for others. When once we begin to see how absolutely indispensable intercession is, just as much a duty as loving God or believing in Christ, and how we are called and bound to it as believers, we shall feel that to cease intercession is grievous sin.

Let us ask for grace to take up our place as priests with joy, and give our life to bring down the blessing of heaven.

ANDREW MURRAY

Sweet Intercessions

Isaac prayed to the LORD on behalf of his wife, because she was barren.
The LORD answered his prayer, and his wife Rebekah became pregnant.

GENESIS 25:21

Lord Jesus,

You invite me to petition You on behalf of my spouse through prayer. With Your disciples, I ask today, "Lord, teach me to pray . . ." (Luke 11:1).

I want to be my partner's trusted intercessor throughout our lives together (1 Sam. 12:23). Bless me with the sincerity and tenacity to be a "prayer striver," as Your Word encourages me to be (Rom. 15:30). This is my duty—and I accept it as my *privilege*. Let my prayers and my love swirl around my mate in one beautiful expression in my marriage.

Right now I especially pray that You will turn the tests my partner will face today into part of Your larger plan for his or her life (Phil. 1:19).

I will do—I Myself will grant —whatever you may ask in My name . . . so that the Father may be glorified (John 14:13, AMP).

Thank You, loving Lord.

Amen.

Praise God and Live

His wife said to him, "Are you still holding on to your integrity? Curse God and die!"

JOB 2:9

A WIFE'S PRAYER

Lord God,
I've never told my husband to curse You and die, but sometimes when he is terribly discouraged or hit hard by a crisis, I don't respond in faith. Rather than encourage my husband to hang on to what he knows is right, I've chosen to comfort myself by taking matters into my own hands—with a charge card, a dangerous line of thinking, or a selfish solution. Forgive me, Lord! I *never* want to be like Job's wife! Help me champion faith and integrity in our marriage, even when evil seems to be winning. Teach me from Your Word the kind of wifely encouragements that will renew my husband's hope:

— "God will never let us be tested beyond our ability to resist. He will always make a way out" (from 1 Cor. 10:13).

— "Remember God's many loving deeds for us" (from Ps. 77:11).

— "Let's put on the full armor of God, and stand our ground" (from Eph. 6:13).

— "We can set our hope fully on the grace that God will give us in Jesus Christ" (from 1 Pet. 1:13).

In a moment of testing today, help me say, "Hang on to Your integrity, Honey. Let's praise God and live!"

Amen.

Suddenly Present

While they were still talking about this, Jesus himself stood among them and said to them, "Peace be with you."

LUKE 24:36

Dear Jesus Christ,

You can make Your presence so real, as You did to Your disappointed followers on the road to Emmaus (Luke 24:13-34), and before that to those frightened fishermen on the stormy lake (John 6:19), and to a grieving Mary in Gethsemane (John 20:11,16).

Appear in our day, in our marriage. Surprise us, most surprising Lord. Suddenly speak into our innermost beings what we need to hear:

You have been joined together in my name—that means I am always here, with you at all times. No one can snatch you away from me (from Matt. 18:20, John 10:28).

Yes, Lord, we believe Your promise to be with us in our marriage always. All day long, help us to recognize Your presence—to see You in the face of a child; through kind words or a tender touch; by an eternal truth remembered; over the kitchen clamor; in that still, small voice; by the comfort and power of Your Holy Spirit . . .

We will remember and watch for You all day. Favor us, dear Lord. We cry out with Moses, "If Your Presence does not go with us, do not send us up from here" (Exod. 33:15).

Amen.

Still More Love

I thank my God for you . . . whenever I think of you. My constant prayers for you are a real joy.

PHILIPPIANS 1:3-4, PH

PRAYING WITH PAUL

Heavenly Father,
Today our prayer is that we may have *still more love* —
a love that is full of knowledge and every wise insight.
Help us to always recognize Your highest
and best for us,
and to live sincere and blameless lives
until the day of Christ.
May our lives be full of true goodness,
produced by the power that Jesus Christ gives us
to the praise and glory of God.
Amen.
(from Phil. 1:9-11, PH)

NOTES

An Invitation

1. David M. Dawson, *More Power in Prayer* (Grand Rapids: Zondervan, 1942), 104.

2. Francois Fénelon, as quoted in *A Guide to Prayer,* ed. Reuben P. Job and Morman Shawchuck (Nashville: Upper Room Books, 1983), 56.

Chapter 1

1. Mike Mason, *The Mystery of Marriage* (Sisters, Ore.: Multnomah, 1985), 91.

2. Antoine de Saint-Exupéry, quoted in Art Hunt, *Praying with the One You Love* (Sisters, Ore.: Multnomah, 1996), 12.

3. Larry Crabb, *The Marriage Builder: A Blueprint for Couples and Counselors* (Grand Rapids: Zondervan, 1982), 63.

4. Warren and Ruth Myers, *31 Days of Prayer* (Sisters, Ore.: Multnomah, 1997), 166-7.

5. Frederick Buechner, quoted in Mary Jenson, *Partners in Promise* (Sisters, Ore.: Multnomah, 1996), 43.

Chapter 2

1. *Book of Common Prayer* (Kingsport, Tenn.: Kingsport Press, 1977), 336.

2. C. S. Lewis, *The Joyful Christian,* quoted in Bob Benson Sr. and Michael W. Benson, *Disciplines for the Inner Life* (Nashville: Generoux/Nelson, 1989), 272.

3. Wayne Spear, *The Theology of Prayer* (Grand Rapids: Baker, 1979), 59-60.

4. Spear, *The Theology of Prayer,* 57.

5. Henri J. M. Nouwen, *With Open Hands* (New York: Ballantine Books/Epiphany, 1985), 3-8.

6. Richard J. Foster, *Prayers from the Heart* (San Francisco: HarperSanFrancisco, 1994), xiv.

Quotations

Oswald Chambers, "God's Workmanship," *Christianity Today*, 4 October 1993, 40.

Richard Foster, *Prayer* (San Francisco: Harper San Francisco, 1992), 184, 179.

Emilie Griffin, "Clinging: The Experience of Prayer," quoted in Bob Benson Sr. and Michael W. Benson, *Disciplines of the Inner Life* (Nashville: Generoux/Nelson, 1989), 287.

Soren Kierkegaard, "Thou God of Love," *The Prayers of Kierkegaard*, ed. Perry D. LeFevre (Chicago: University of Chicago Press, 1963), 11.

Mike Mason, *The Mystery of Marriage* (Sisters, Ore.: Multnomah, 1996), 163.

Thomas Merton, *No Man Is an Island* (New York: Image Books, 1967), 19, 20.

Andrew Murray, *The Ministry of Intercession,* in *The Andrew Murray Collection* (Ulrichsville, Ohio: Barbour, 1954), 3.

Henri J. Nouwen, "The Genesee Diary," quoted in Bob Benson Sr. and Michael W. Benson, *Disciplines of the Inner Life* (Nashville: Generoux/Nelson, 1989), 105.

Spanish liturgy, quoted in Vinita Hampton Wright, *Prayers Across the Centuries* (Wheaton, Ill.: Harold Shaw, 1993), 67.

Mother Teresa, *Heart of Joy* (Ann Arbor, Mich.: Servant Books, 1987), 105.

Paul Tournier, quoted in Bill Carmichael, *7 Habits of a Healthy Home* (Wheaton, Ill.: Tyndale, 1997), 154.

William Butler Yeats, quoted in H. Jackson Brown Jr., *On Love* (Nashville: Rutledge Hill Press, 1995).

Title Index

Topical Index